MW00626072

AMERICA

(USA)

IN PURSUIT OF FREEDOM
AND JUSTICE

BY

DIMITRIOS K. KAKAVITSAS

America (USA) In Pursuit of Freedom and Justice

Copyright © 2010

Dimitrios K. Kakavitsas

First Edition

ISBN 978-0-615-39266-0

Poplar Street Press

www.poplarstreetpress.com

Printed in the United States of America. No part of this book may be used or reproduced in any manner whatsoever without written permission of the publisher except in the case of brief quotations embodied in critical articles and reviews.

Dedication

This book is dedicated to my family and all those who believed in me and helped me see a ray of sunshine in the middle of this relentless storm and in the adverse circumstances, try to see my potential and to estimate my limits.

Contents

Note from the Publisher

A small and brief preface to the things herein, written by an immigrant transplanted from a distant Greek province to the country with the most progressive technological development, evolution in communications and administrative structure, definitely is a surprise and at the same time causes admiration and disappointment.

Disappointment for the the lack of affection of this great nation of the United States of America towards its citizens and about the total disregard for the principles of justice and of democracy, established by its pioneers presidents such as George Washington, John Adams, Thomas Jefferson James Madison, Abraham Lincoln and later Dwight Eisenhower and John F. Kennedy. This country was established by the men who were inspired by the principles of justice and democracy, from the cradle of law and democracy, Greece.

The contemporary times though, the technology and the fear of the diffusion of drugs and terrorism have made the government a 'blind mechanism' to the point that it lacks consideration of its humanistic past and barricades itself behind tough and cruel laws and behind excessive police authority.

It made itself disrespect the 'family asylum' and the 'professional asylum' of its citizens and made the justice system agree inconsiderably and uncritically with the suggestions of the persecuting authorities and to mercilessly pass down penalties and imprisonments to citizens who have been falsely accused as agitators of the public order and security of the country so that they serve prison sentences for many years.

The author of this book, a victim of the atmosphere that reigns all over the United States, raises a voice of concern and gives a determined notice against the *status quo* and also gently asks the responsible political agents to amend and modernize the legal context of the justice system. The system which governs these imprisonments needs to be humanized.

We strongly believe that the people who read this book will sympathize with the author, an immigrant in the land of freedom and justice, who received a severe blow to his reputation by his imprisonment in an American prison after being falsely accused.

The author unfolds in the most sincere and spontaneous way his experience, recites his complaints in a dramatic way and makes an appeal to the legislators to amend the legal framework around which the system of criminal justice revolves.

Moreover, the things that this immigrant points out are things that public men and women have suggested before him without yet being heard.

America now needs to be invested not only with the prestige of technology and space research and the development of science, but also with the robe of culture and the prevalence of humanistic principles if it really desires to pave the road as the leading country of the world.

The Publisher.

Preface

When the following day comes when I'm gone and I'm not close to you all, to see you, when the sun rises and it finds your eyes full of tears for me, how much I wish you all not cry the way you cried out, once you realized how many things we still had to live for together.

I do know how much you all love me as much as I love you too.

I do know every single minute you are thinking of me and how much you miss me. When the next morning comes and you're without me, please try to understand that some people called my name and told me that my cell is ready and that I should go and dwell there, away from all of you, away from all the people and the things I loved so much and still love. I'm being truthful. When I turned around to follow them and left you all, my knees gave out beneath me.

My heart sank and my eyes flooded with tears for all those that I left behind.

I didn't want to say goodbye and didn't want to go to prison without being a criminal. I still had so many things to live for and do. I begged the government not to take me from you all. I asked them to let me clean up the streets and I would give any money I'd earn to the poor. But this plea fell on deaf ears. I thought that all this was just a bad dream. But when I passed the iron gate of prison with my hands in chains, I accepted the fact I was a convict.

My life stopped there and all my dreams were left at the front door.

Introduction

Every creature has a Creator. A creature is always a result of an action of its creator. Nothing can speak by itself. Airplanes cannot say, "We created ourselves so we are the creators of ourselves."

The creatures of God in nature and in the universe show His wisdom and His omnipotence. The same happens with humans. This book is a creature. It's a true story that shows the bitterness and pain of a poor boy who migrated to America in 1967 to find a better future and a better life.

After 40 years of hard work and effort, this unjust system and its organizers with numerous lies took the wages of his life and put him and his son in prison.

This poor child now makes an appeal to all the big politicians of the USA to amend the laws and help millions of people who are in prison without having committed a crime; to revise all judicial decisions that resolve around petty offenses, false accusations, false witnesses and unyielding judges supposedly attached to the laws. But the laws are unjust and too harsh. He begs all the judges not to pass down such severe sentences.

While he is in prison the author writes about his life, his childhood and his common life with the Greek artists. He also writes about many problems on earth, including AIDS.

He thanks all people who helped him out in his deep suffering and finished the book by sharing a couple of jokes and proverbs with you, the reader.

Figure 1 - The Author as a youth

My Childhood

I was born in 1952, in Neohori, Eurytanias region. Neohori was a small but very beautiful village in a beautiful meadow surrounded by beautiful hills between two wonderful rivers, Megdova and Agrafiotis. My family was big: the parents, eight children and the grandmother. I had an older sister therefore I was the second child.

I was the oldest son so I had to help everywhere.

Since I started walking for the first time I was always around the sheep with my grandmother. I remember once we were in the middle of the meadow with my grandma and I was very hungry; so somewhere she found an egg and fried it in a small pan without any oil. I held a hood above the pan because it was raining and that's how she kept the fire going.

I remember I could not go back home from the meadow at night because it was about 2 hours away and uphill. My father would come down and then would put me on his shoulders, piggyback, under his long overcoat. I used to hold him around his neck all the way back home.

Our lunch was the same every day. I had an onion, cornbread, and a few olives.

When I turned 7, I had to go to school because it was mandatory. Thankfully it was mandatory because otherwise I don't think I would ever have attended. So I had to go to school every day and help my father with all his chores. Many times he didn't let me go to school because he needed me to tend to the sheep. Back in those days we didn't have any books and whatever we learned depended on the teacher who wrote the lessons on the board.

I remember one day the teacher asked me to come to the board and solve a math problem he had solved the previous day while I was absent. Obviously, I couldn't solve it so he asked me to extend and open my hand so he could discipline me with a ruler. As he raised the ruler, I got scared and pulled my hand back causing him to hit his leg. Very angrily the teacher brought a stone from outside and rubbed it on the ground to make it sharp. He forced me to kneel on it. I stayed there until my knees started bleeding. Then he kicked me and I fell on the desks.

When the class was over I rushed to my father, crying, showed him my knees and told him about how the teacher had kicked me. Then he hugged me and promised me that he would talk to the teacher.

After a week, in a parent-teacher meeting, my father confronted the teacher, "Dear teacher, we raise our children with many struggles and we send them to school because we want them to learn, not for you to play soccer with them."

The teacher turned red and the only thing he said

was, "I try to make them learn."

Then my father said, "Let them learn as much as they can. They won't become prime ministers!"

After that the teacher never hit me again but to get even, he gave my sister failing grades. Even though she was a much better student than I, she failed the class.

One day I was at the meadow with the sheep and the teacher sent my sister there to pick me up and bring me to school. Our father then told her to stay at the meadow with the sheep as well. That's how I finished Elementary school.

Back then many kids in my village filled out applications to go to repair workshops sponsored by the Queen (Technical Education of Queen Frederica) somewhere in Peloponnesus so they can learn a craft. I wanted to go too, but I couldn't. I knew how much my father needed me. When I asked him, he said, "It would be very nice if you went, but who would stay with the sheep?"

Figure 2 - The Author, 8 yrs old, with lambs in his village in Greece

At the time my father made a trade with someone and exchanged his sheep for goats. At the same time he bought 80 more goats so now he had 160. I still remember, when he brought them, they weren't familiar with each other so they started hitting each other. I was put in charge of the goats when I was 12 and my father took upon himself all the other duties and the agricultural tasks.

Those days, agricultural work was hard because everything was done by hand. Whoever would fill up their storage with corn would be considered the rich ones. I remember the horses plowing the meadows and the peeling of the corn. The moon shined bright in the sky and we sang all night long. Those nights were like perfect dreams that we won't ever live again.

Several times I used to take the mule and go tend to the goats. I loaded it with wood and milk to please my mother so that she might secretly give me an extra egg to eat. She always would hide the eggs in the corn storage. I remember once I went back home and before unloading the wood, I asked my mother if the food was ready.

"A couple of minutes ago I sent your sister Maria to the fountain to bring some water to make some bean soup," she said.

Figure 3 - The Water Fountain at the Village

When I heard that, I started taking the mule back to where I got the wood from. Then she said, "Bring the wood here and I'll fry two eggs for you."

Once, after I had milked the goats, I put the jar of milk under a tree because I had to lead the goats up the mountain. When I got back, I saw a snake drinking my milk.

I got scared and started throwing rocks at it. The snake had already drunk half of the milk and I didn't know what to do to avoid trouble with my mother. Many times she waited for the milk to boil and serve it to the entire family. I thought of what to do. I went to the village, looked around, and nobody was there. I finished filling the jar with water and went back home. Before my mother started boiling it she added more water and diluted it. Anyway, everyone drank from the milk except my father. When he put a spoonful in his mouth, he said, "This is not milk. It's water."

Then my mother told him, "Come on now. The milk is fine. It's all in your head."

Then I thought, 'everything will be ok.'

I remember the pants I used to wear. You couldn't see their true color because of the many patches they had. I was 9 then. My father bought my first shoes, called "rubbers." Back then people didn't buy shoes according to the size but according to the age of the child. You went to the store, told the clerks the age of the child and they'd give you the shoes. In the village there was no store like that so we had to go to the city. I guess I was small for my age and that's why my shoes were always too big.

Figure 4 - The Author with his brother and his father in USA - 1970

My father was my whole life because he loved us very much. I remember one day he sent me to the village next to ours to buy some house supplies. When I came back, one of my cousins told me: "I'm going to the Festival in Magoula. I want to sell some of my pigs. Do you want to come with me and help? I'll pay you."

When I heard about the Festival, without even asking my father's permission, I said 'ok'. I wanted to take some food with me but he said that I didn't need to because he had food for me. He was walking in front and I was following behind, pushing the pigs to make them walk. After five hours of walking, we stopped at a fountain behind Tatarna place. There he took out a couple of olives and some bread from his bag. He ate them all and then we continued on our way.

Around nightfall we arrived at Magoula. He made a temporary sheepfold and put me in charge of the pigs. He picked out a pig, then he roasted it and sold it. Around 11 at night I went close to him because I thought he might give me something to eat, but he gave me nothing. I was embarrassed to ask him for food so I fell asleep next to the pigs with an empty stomach. The next day, after I realized that I would not eat again, I left the pigs and went to the Festival. One of our neighbors and relative was there. He used to go there every year and open a restaurant three months before the Festival began. He was a nice man that rescued me. When I got into his restaurant, his wife asked me whether I was hungry but I said 'no' because I was embarrassed and I didn't have any money. I wished she would have asked me again.

Then her husband came over and said, "Why are you asking him? Don't you see that the boy is starving?"

Then he took the top of the pan, filled it with spaghetti, and that's how I survived that day.

When I got back all the pigs were gone. They had gone to the Acheloos River. I rushed there but I didn't see the river flowing and I almost drowned. I thought that it was a muddy land but afterwards I realized that it was a river. With a lot of struggling, I led the pigs to the sheep fold one by one.

I survived the next night with spaghetti. The third day I was really hungry. I realized that the guy who had the pigs would never give me any food so I decided to leave the pigs and go back to my village.

I ran into two kids who were passing on a horse and I begged them to take me with them to Tatarna and to show me the way back to the village. I would have left earlier but I didn't know how to get back home.

We were going up a hill and I saw the tail end of my father's horse disappearing behind a turn in the road. It was my father who was going to the Festival of Magoula. Once I saw him I started crying and he took me in his arms. Then he said to me those words that, whenever I hear them, they make my heart ache: "Didn't I tell you never to leave my side?"

After that he took me piggyback and we went back to the Festival. He rushed immediately to that guy and told him, "Shame on you! You took a little kid with you, away from his home, and gave him nothing to eat."

Then that guy took a coin out of his pocket and gave it to me, but my father took the coin and threw it back at him.

I remember I was always anxious for Christmas to

come. If we had pork I would take the pig's stomach and blow it up like a balloon. Then we would play soccer with it. On Easter I used to make a basket out of wood and decorate it with beautiful flowers from the two pear trees in our garden. I took the basket and went from house to house, knocked on the doors and sang the song *"today the sky is dark."* I came back home with my basket full of eggs, candies and marshmallows.

As I remember we never roasted a lamb on Easter because we used to sell all our sheep to buy other things. I still remember when my father would send me to a store in Sidera. I had a specific notebook for my purchases and I used to buy goods on credit. When I got there I gave my small notebook to the owner of the store and he asked me if my father had given me any money. I said 'no'. He would shake his head and start putting the items in the bags. I don't remember him ever refusing to give me what my father had written in the notebook.

Figure 5 - The Author with his Father in USA - 1974

He was a nice person with a good heart. His last name was Koukounias and I wish all the best to him. We owed him 15,000 drachmas in 1963, which was a lot of money. When my father realized that he couldn't pay him back, he told him to come visit him at the village and my father would give him one of our olive tree fields. When he came to the village and we went to show him the field, my grandmother burst into tears because she didn't want to give it up. He felt sorry for her and said to my father,

"Kosta, let it go. Maybe someday you'll pay me."

Finally in 1965 the Lake of Kremasta was created by compulsory expropriation and many people received other properties somewhere else in exchange. We got money from the flooded fields and that's how we repaid that good man.

My father was very generous and open-handed when he had money and never said 'no' to anyone.

In 1965, my father visited me on a hill where our goats were grazing. He brought me food. It was sleeting and I wore a coat with a hood.

"Take off the hood. I've got news for you," he said.

I took off the hood so I could hear him and he said, "On Christmas I received a letter from my brother in America. He wants to know if we want him to invite us to come to the United States."

I asked him what he was thinking and at first he didn't want to go there. After long and thoughtful consideration and because of the fact that we owed a lot of money to many people, we decided to go to America for five years. We thought we would make some money and then come back to Greece.

Unfortunately, I hadn't heard the song that Stelios Kazantzidis sings:

"Of the ten men who migrate, only one of them succeeds and the others get lost."

One year after that I met my father in the same place. I said to him, "Do you remember what we were talking about last year? What happened with the invitation?"

"We'll know around Christmas," he said.

My uncle used to send us a card every Christmas and Easter. He would put a dollar in the envelope. I liked the color of the dollar. How could I know in those days how much pain and suffering this dollar would cause? When I was a kid I considered money as 'colored paper'.

How could I ever imagine that my uncle lived all

alone in a foreign country far away from his family? I wonder how many dishes he washed in order to earn a dollar.

Finally we got the letter and the card in which my uncle wrote that he had made the invitation for us.

In 1967, after we had finished all of the paperwork, we went to Athens to take the necessary medical tests. It was just two weeks before the dictatorship of Papadopoulos. We finished all the things we were supposed to do in Athens and went back to our village. We sold our goats for 150 drachmas each and that's how we bought the airplane tickets.

We came to Charlotte, NC, in 1967. The people who came to America were my father and I, my sister and two of our uncles with their older children. My uncle found a house and we all lived there together.

The next day we all started looking for jobs. The oldest ones found something right away. Some of them had to wash dishes and some others had to work as busboys. My cousin and I were only 15 years old and nobody wanted to hire us.

One day one of my cousins gave us a ride to a restaurant where the owners were three brothers from Arahova of Peloponnesus. He begged the oldest owner, Sotiris Kopsiaftis, to give us jobs so that we might survive.

Mr. Kopsiaftis was a very nice man and many Greek people found a job there. He looked at me and said, "If you promise me that you won't cut off your fingers in the kitchen, I'll hire you."

I said "ok", so he led me to the kitchen. He showed me how I could wear a kitchen apron. He put a hat on my head and brought me a stool to step on so I could reach the onion slicer.

Figure 6 - The Author working in a kitchen

He showed me how to slice them and make onion rings.

He had also hired my cousin, but I don't think that we worked together. The only thing I remember is that when he paid us, I got 17 dollars and my cousin got only 16.

"I got paid more money," I said, "Because I'm better than you."

When I sliced the onions I couldn't see because of the tears in my eyes. I didn't know that a person could have so many tears, to be crying the entire day and not running out of tears.

When that day was over and the time came for me to leave work, a young fellow showed me where to get the bus to go home. He said, "You'll take bus number 2 uptown. Then you'll get bus number 11 and when you get close to your place, you pull the string and the driver will stop the bus and let you out."

I understood as much as I could but there was nothing else I could do but follow his instructions. I got in the bus and when I got uptown, I saw two buses with the same number 11. The first was heading in one direction and the second in the opposite direction. I had no idea which bus to take so I decided to get on one of those two with my eyes closed and let my fortune guide me. People were getting on and off, but I felt like a permanent resident of the bus.

It was after midnight and the bus had made its last stop. The driver got out of the bus, so I had to get out too. I had no clue as to where to go. It was freezing and all the places around me looked the same. I went to a gas station and burst into tears. A police car stopped next to me and the officer said something to me but I didn't understand it. I handed him a paper where my address was written. Then he gave me a ride to my place, which means that there are some courteous police officers out there.

The next day I tried to go to work, but again I had nothing but difficulties. I got to work two hours late with tears in my eyes and the fear that my boss would fire me. When I got in there he calmed me down and suggested that he might give me a ride to work every morning and his brother would give me a ride home every night. I was very relieved and didn't even think of the endless hours I'd be spending in the restaurant every day.

One day, while I was preparing chickens, I saw that they threw away the necks and the entrails. I asked the boss if I could have them. That's how we secured our daily meal. So every single day we knew what dish we would have for dinner: chicken necks with rice.

Our only problem was that we didn't have any plates so we had to eat directly from the pot one by one. One day a Greek friend came over to visit us and my sister told him, "I have good food, but I don't have any plates to serve you. If you want to eat you'll have to eat from the pot." Then he took my father and one of my uncles and left. When they came back, they brought every kitchen supply we needed from his restaurant. His name was Menios Balatsias and he was a good man as well.

After about a year the cook who prepared the food left, so I asked the boss if he would give me the cook's job. I wanted to stop washing dishes. At first the boss thought that I wouldn't make it, but he decided to give me a try. I had learned everything just by watching the cook prepare the portions people ordered. Even if I couldn't read English, I was able to recognize what was written on the packages by just looking at the labels. He put me in this position and I was really fast. I prepared everything and then waited for the next order. Once the job started, the place was overwhelmed by orders. I did everything well. I waited until the orders were picked up before placing new ones on the board. Then I heard the boss saying to another boy, "Go take Mitro's position." The boss used to call me by the nickname 'Mitros.' When he came and told me to go back to washing dishes I burst into tears because I felt I was being replaced for no good reason.

The boss saw me sighing with despair and said, "Mitros, stay in your cooking position and nobody should bother you again." I was very relieved that I wasn't demoted that day. I worked there for two years until I met Panagioti Politis. He had a restaurant and suggested that I might work for him under better conditions.

Don't misunderstand me when I say "to work for him." In those days we used to talk like that. Now things have changed and people say "I work for myself."

How can you say that you work for yourself when

you work under other people's authority who dictate what you do?

I wanted to quit my job but I was embarrassed to tell my boss. Finally I left the job without telling him.

After one year I called him to ask for a loan and once he picked up the phone he recognized me immediately. When he asked me how I was doing, I said, "I'm sorry. The reason I left without saying a word was that I was embarrassed to talk to you."

He said, "Never mind that" and asked me if I needed something.

I asked him to lend me $5,000 to open a restaurant and he replied, "Come over this Monday and get it."

I was so shocked because I didn't expect him to agree. Five thousand dollars was a huge amount of money back then. Somehow I never ended up needing to borrow the money from him, but it was the same as if he had loaned me the money. I want to thank all those people from the bottom of my heart who helped me make a living and feed my family. I don't agree with people who say employers take advantage of us. We all reserve the right to leave a job if we don't like it.

In 1968, my father went to Greece for my sister's wedding. I was left alone in America. I remember, when I came back from work at night, I would look underneath beds and inside closets to see if there were any burglars in our home.

Then I got very homesick thinking of my village, my parents, my brothers and the nice things I had left behind. It was torture for me living away from home. My dream was to save some money, buy a new car, and then go back to my village.

In 1970, I turned 18 and with the help of a Greek friend I got a driver's license. I bought my first car for $500 on good terms from a friend of mine. The first day I got the car I took my brother and sister down to the river. Also, I stopped taking the bus everywhere. My father used to come from Greece and leave again because he didn't like America. I didn't like it either but I didn't have any other choice. So I became the leader of my family. I always worked two jobs to make a living for all of us and I sent most of the money to my father.

I saved $1,000 and went to Greece. Then I had to borrow money to buy the return ticket. My nostalgia and homesickness were always uncured wounds in my heart.

In 1972, I received a letter from my father saying that in the village Loutra of Kremasta he met an orphan girl who was poor and very beautiful. Her father had drowned when she was four years old. She sent me her picture. We sent each other a couple of letters and that was it. Her brother George said to my father, "We don't like the whole situation, letters and stuff. When your son comes back from America then we can discuss this again."

Her brother gave everything for his brother and sisters. That's how he earned my respect for life.

In 1973, when I went to Greece, I went with my

By Dimitrios K. Kakavitsas

family to meet this girl. They knew that we would visit them but they had no idea when we were coming. They lived far away. There were no telephone lines in that area and we had to go to their home on foot. When we arrived at their home in the mountains, her sister came out of the house and called the girl, who was planting onions, to come into the house. They were friendly and made us feel welcome. The only person who was missing was her father. I was saddened by the fact that her father couldn't see his daughter and feel proud of her at her wedding.

They prepared a wonderful dinner and asked me what I thought about the girl.

Error

37

Figure 7 - The Author - First meeting with his wife - 1973 in Greece

I was then 21 years old and kind of shy but I told them that the girl was exceptional and I was interested in her. She went outside for a while to the yard with her mother and sister. When she came back, she said "Yes." She had made the big decision to trust me and marry me.

Then her brother told me that the girl had a dowry of 80,000 drachmas and if I wanted I might add 80,000 more drachmas so we could buy a piece of land in the town of Agrinio. I had no money, not even for a honey-moon. I told him, "If you like, give us 30,000 drachmas for our honeymoon expenses until we leave for America and give your other sister the remaining 50,000 drachmas as a dowry."

The next day I went back to my village to meet my Godmother, whom I had never met. My father had told me that my Godmother was a witch and could break spells. My parents had lost three babies before I was born. Somebody told my father to go to Sardinia, close to Amphilohia, and find that woman. When he got there, she told him he was cursed to lose all of his children. She said, "Your wife is pregnant with a boy. When she gives birth to the boy, take the baby and bring it to me to bapt-ize him." My father agreed and she baptized me when I was born.

After the baptism, my father never lost another child.

I wanted her to marry us so I went to Agrinio,

bought some gifts and went to Sardinia to find my God-mother. I asked the people around where the house of Mrs. Papanikou was. I found it and when I knocked on the door, she came to the door. She was 80 years old at the time and I told her I was getting married and I asked her to marry us. She was very glad to hear it and said 'yes.' She gave me two lucky charms and said to me, "You should always wear one of them and your fiancé should wear the other one." I didn't be-lieve in witchcraft and I told her that. Then she said, "It doesn't matter that you don't believe, but you should wear it anyway. I break spells. This means that somebody else is mak-ing them."

I took the charms, said goodbye to her and left. When we set the date for the wedding, I went again to her house to tell her the wedding date. When I got there, I saw a black rib-bon on her door and realized that my Godmother had died.

After the wedding ceremony we went for a stroll in Kerkira and then left for America.

Figure 8 - The Wedding Day

In 1974 our first son, Kostas, was born and in 1976 we had our second son, Vasilis.

Figure 9 - The Wedding Day with Family

Figure 10 - The Author with his wife and son - 1978

I tried several times to go back to Greece for good, but the political situation didn't allow me to stay there.

In 1976, I felt fed up with living abroad and I was homesick. So I said to myself, I will work in my homeland and I will live how the other 10 million Greeks live. I didn't have a lot of money, only about $3,000.

I went to Lamia city and bought an ouzo tavern close to the Park Square for $2,500. I worked from 4 am until 2 am but it didn't matter to me. I was really happy to hear people speaking my language.

**Figure 11 - The Author with his wife and two sons, Kosta and Vasili -
1985**

I had applied for a business license so I could open
the tavern. A police officer called me and said, "I am sorry, but I cannot give you a license for this place." I didn't
know much, plus I was intimidated by his rank, so I believed him. He also said, "You have only three weeks to
leave the place, otherwise we will close it." I had just

bought a refrigerator for $600 on credit.

I finally sold the ouzo tavern to somebody for $600 only to pay off the refrigerator. I gave him the tavern and left thinking that I fooled him. From there I went with my wife to Agrinio city where I couldn't find a job, so I left again for America.

After one year, I went back to Greece and passed through Lamia just to take a look at the old places. I even passed by the ouzo tavern and it was crowded.

Then I took a breath and went in. Once the owner saw me, he greeted me and said, "You saved me with this tavern. You gave me the opportunity to have a home." I congratulated him and asked him if he had any problem with the license and then he replied, "When I first came here, I was told that the place should have two toilets and other stuff. When they finished, I gave them $300 and they gave me the license."

Then I realized what's going on and said, "I wish I knew this in the first place. I would have given double the money."

In 1979, I got back to Greece having $10,000. I went to Agrinio and bought an apartment. After that I found a place to open a tavern. Then I went to the police department and they gave me a list of things I needed to do to get a license. I prepared everything to the point where I also put in a mosaic floor. When I finished everything I went to the police again and told them the tavern was ready for inspection. They said: "We will not give you a license for this place because the landlord of the tavern supported the Communist Party in Greece."

The next day I went to the police again and they told me to open the restaurant and they would come to inspect it. I asked the officer if I might open it without having a license and he said 'yes' because it would take six months for me to get the license.

The night of the grand opening the inspectors came over and asked me to show them the license. I told them what exactly the police officer had told me, but they replied, "According to the law you are not allowed to open a store without a license. You have to close it."

"Now I've already opened it," I said, "so I can't close it."

They gave me a ticket and left. After a month, a guy from the health department came over. After he found everything in proper order, he said to me, "You know, the ceiling is low, so I can't give you a license."

Then I remember the 'ouzo tavern' in Lamia. "Never mind," I said, "here is $300 to have a drink on me. Send me the license by mail."

That's how I overcame the problem with the license.

Figure 12 - The Author with his father in Greece - 1995

When October came I didn't have much business so I decided to go to my village. I took a lamb from my father to roast it on a spit and sell it in order to pay the rent. Once I put it on the spit, some inspectors came over again and asked where I got the lamb from. I told them the truth and they gave me a ticket again.

When I came to the point of having 5 or 6 tickets, I closed the restaurant because if I went to court, I would owe more than $10,000 and I didn't have any money. I looked for a job but found nothing. I gathered olives, I worked in a warehouse, but all the jobs I found were part-time.

After that I was unemployed again. I had only $3.00 in my pocket. I went to a grocery store, bought 8 packages of spaghetti and brought them to my wife. I told her to cook a half of a package at noon and the other half at night. I was looking for $10 to go to Athens by bus. There I would find my friend Chris Stremenos, who might buy me a ticket to America. Everything ended up being the way I had imagined it.

When I came to Charlotte NC, I rushed to Kostas Balis and told him, "Kosta, my family will starve if I don't send them money immediately. Please, lend me $1,000 so I can send it to them and once I start working, I'll pay you off."

Without saying a word he gave me a check and he also bought the plane tickets for my wife and my children. After 15 days they came to America.

Figure 13 - The Author with his sister and brothers

In 1983 I was sitting at the kitchen table with my wife. Our children were playing on the floor and talking to each other in English. I did not hear one Greek word. I told my wife, "After a while, when the children grow up, we won't be able to communicate with them."

"That's true, but what can we do?" she said.

"Let's get ready to go back to Greece and they might go to school there to learn Greek," I answered.

After one month we arrived at Agrinio, Greece, again. Across from our apartment there was a kafenió. I started hanging out there until I found out what to do. The police saw me there but they had no idea who I was.

One afternoon somebody knocked on the door of our house. I opened the door and a policeman asked me: "Are you Kakavitsas?"

"Yes. Why?" I said.

"You failed to appear in court three years ago so I have to place you under arrest," he said.

"You don't need to make any effort to arrest me," I said. "I will come with you willingly,"

When we arrived at the police station they gave me some papers and I paid $2,000.

Our children started to go to public school on a regular basis. After Greek school, they went to English school and then the Greek teacher would take them to her house and teach them Greek again.

One day, while I was sitting in a kafenió having

coffee, a man came over and asked me, "Who are you? I know all people here, but I don't know you."

I told him that I just came from America and he asked me what my job was. I told him that I didn't have a job and he said, "You seem to be a nice person, pretty qualified, and I have a great idea for you. My brother and I have that store across the street and we have many customers from the Mesologgi area who come over here and purchase car paint from us. The name of the paint company is Sickens. Do you want to go to Mesologgi and open a store like that and sell paint?"

I agreed and everything went as planned. These two brothers were Andreas and Spyros Raptis.

We lived in Agrinio very well for three years. Our children learned Greek and we all enjoyed our beloved homeland which we had missed so much in the past.

Figure 14 - The Author with his wife on Easter Day in USA

I was 35 years old and the money I earned was just enough to survive. I could not see any future there, so I decided again to come back to America for a better life. In 1986 I finally decided to stay in America permanently.

Once I came back to America, I got a phone call from Panagiotis Politis, who said, "Welcome back Dimitri. If you want you can come and work for me." I felt it was time for me to open my own business. "I told him,

"If you truly want us to work together, make me a partner."

The next day he called me and said 'ok'. I didn't have any cash, so I rushed to my friends to borrow some money. In January of 1988, Politis and I became partners. In 1993 we sold that restaurant and opened my current restaurant. Politis eventually retired and left the restaurant.

Figure 15 - The Author with Sue Myrick, Mayor of Charlotte in 1988

Figure 16 - The Author with his father at their village in Greece

I worked very hard the last years to help my son finish Law School. I built a shopping center and our dream-house, which my wife and I had been dreaming about for a long time. All these things were built with loans and the sweat of an entire lifetime.

I was planning for our children to get married and settle down so we'd be very proud of them. We were planning for and expecting better days.

I felt I had accomplished something important in

my life. Our dreams had come true, but the ugly side of fate had other plans for us.

I could not have ever imagined that the government, with its power and all those lies, might come and take everything from us, destroy us and throw us in prison. I've seen a lot of illusions in this world. We live in a real jungle where the stronger animal devours the weaker one.

In December 2002, on a morning of freezing rain, they brought darkness and pain to my home. Where love was dwelling some starless night, the pain was piling high.

I am waiting in agony until April 17, 2006, to get out of prison and live again with great joy and be with my loved ones. I want to see those who really love me and suffered my pain, again.

Figure 17 - The Author

The Prisons are Overflowing

My beloved friends, I welcome you with all my love and appreciation and I hope my book finds you in great health and peace.

I thank you for holding this book in your hands. I want you to keep in mind that books should have essential content and narrate something important. Only then will the words flow freely. This book was written under bad circumstances, under great suffering, pain and grief, which weighed down on me and my entire family.

In this book you'll learn things that no one can imagine. I want you to know that our people suffer greatly from the lack of justice and the cruelty of the current system. I'm telling you nothing but the truth and I feel deep pain in my heart because I can't speak to you words of joy and happiness.

I wish that we lived in a society of honesty, where the sun would shine every day for everybody and that all people would share in its bright light. Unfortunately, that is something that doesn't exist nowadays.

For my whole life I've been fighting hard for a better future, a future which anybody might expect. With 'clean hands' and 'head up', I thought I had made it and that the flow of the river could not change. In an instant my expectations got shattered and the flow of the river did divert and headed back up the mountain.

Speech can be joyful and painful. One speech carries a smile and the other bitterness. One brings the lies and the phony image, the other the depth and the truth. The emotional speech always reveals the boundaries of life. Those boundaries need to be protected from the threat of insanity and deception.

The goal of this book is to uncover the fraud, to lighten the dark roots and to lead people to brighter horizons so that they can keep fighting for a better 'tomorrow.'

We all know that only humans are capable of skepticism because on earth they have a conscience. Only humans can wonder about our beginning, the structure, and the purpose of the Universe. Only humans are struggling to answer the questions that still torment our planet. Only the human species discusses the issues of liberty, justice, truth, reason, life and death.

My beloved friends, what I think is this: the animals do not have worries. They only eat, drink and die. Alas! If humans only acted like animals, then it wouldn't be worthwhile to live at all. Human life means to fight, struggle, and progress to the never-failing Light, even if we have, nowadays, the motto, *no problem.*

Unfortunately, the problems are many. Yesterday is always better than today. Our planet suffers from the lack of proper leadership. Those who need to be heard don't talk and if somebody decides to speak and tell the truth, the others call them 'insane.' There's no justice and compassion anywhere. Everything is organized automatically, as if it were a robot. It's not humans that judge any more but the newspapers and the books.

So the judges tell you: "You are right, but our sentencing guidelines suggest 5 to10 years in prison." The laws are written down, but the judge is the one who has to determine if you are really guilty.

The only one who does whatever he likes is the District Attorney. This individual is your biggest enemy. He's the one who led you there with innumerable lies and he now tries to convict you for as many crimes as he can. In the District Attorney's eyes, all citizens are criminals and that's how he/she makes a living. Those people don't work to bring justice. Their only goal is to send you to prison for as many years as possible. Instead of having a system of Justice on our side as a protector, we have it working against us. Instead of giving people education, the system chooses to build more prisons even though there is still 35% illiteracy among American people.

There are no more rights left to the American citizens. They've lost them all. Nobody has a deep perspective of what is really going on. The laws are relentless and destructive towards citizens, truly harsh. Edward Kennedy called this system of justice, "destructive." Since then nothing has changed and everything is getting worse. Injustice and strife prevail everywhere. Every day people are ruined and families are destroyed.

Why do we keep criticizing mistakes without doing something to correct them? This *status quo* cannot function. It's convenient for a few but destroys a lot of people. We are used to living under the threat of terrorism so that the system passes laws against us and the citizens are afraid to speak. The Patriot Act has given the police all the authority to enter your house whenever they want and do whatever they like without asking. And if they don't like your face, they may plant some drugs in your home and send you to prison for 20 years. The laws with regard to racketeering and conspiracy can send entire families to prison. If five people hang out somewhere together the police may accuse them of being 'crime organizers' and arrest them.

The laws against drugs in America are the harshest laws in the entire world. Trains and ships carry the drugs into this country. People with power make a lot of money and then the poor and uneducated people sell them in the streets. Once they make a few dollars the police arrest them, take everything from them and imprison them for 25 years.

That's why I want to ask the judges of America to be less harsh in their sentencing guidelines. The law called "RICO" was passed in 1970 and until 1980 was never used. In 1980 the government put this law in use against five families in New York City that were involved in the 'Mafia' because the 'big bosses' used to bring some Italians into the country for their dirty businesses and the bosses couldn't be touched. According to the RICO law, if you are related to someone who was involved in a crime you would automatically be presumed guilty. Even if you had never been involved in a crime, you could be charged with "conspiracy" anyway.

By enforcing this law, all bosses got arrested and were sent to prison. I read in a newspaper from 1985, which a friend of mine gave me, the story of John Gotti and Spyros Sakaflias. John Gotti won his case four times in a court of law, but the fifth time he lost and was sentenced to life in prison. He later died in prison. Spyros Sakaflias, on the other hand, didn't compromise or take a plea bargain that called for an eight-year prison term. What possibly happened was that his lawyer made a deal with the district attorneys or was incompetent for trial. Incompetence is highly unlikely. His lawyer suggested that he go to trial and he would win the case.

How can this ever happen? To beat the government? Even if you might win once, they will send you to court again and again until they convict you. Sakaflias went to court, lost and was sentenced to life in prison. So after this big success and the effective results of the RICO law, they got excited! The entire system and the police have started using this law everywhere. According to the RICO law, they can charge you with anything and tear you down. They can arrest you on 10 different false charges and each one of them could be punishable up to 20 years imprisonment. They destroy you and then finally tell you: "You have to accept a deal of 5-10 years imprisonment and we promise to drop the other charges." If you refuse to do so, they simply tell you: "if you don't compromise, then we'll put your entire family in prison." And they do that with no problem because they've got the power and account to no one.

I'll ask a simple question: "When they accuse you of 10 charges, how can they drop 9 of them?"

The answer is easy: "Because you haven't done any of them."

My friends, there is a guy named Sammy Gravano (the Bull), the 'deputy chief' for John Gotti, who used to murder in cold blood. After he collaborated with the police, he only got five years in prison plus he received complete protection by the authorities.

So, little by little, we got to this point, to this tragedy. The tragedy of counting over 3 million people in prison, 5 million people on probation and over 40 million people have been labeled as felons.

Today, September 16, 2005, I heard on the radio that in 2004, 4 million people were sentenced to prison in America. If this is true, then things are far worse than described in this book.

There's only one hope: instead of giving you 15% credit for good time, they should give you 50%. Only this way can thousands of people who are now in prison under false charges be able to go back home to their families. They'll pick up the pieces left behind and try to restore their lives. As far as the real criminals, I don't think that there's anybody who wants them to be free. All those people who steal and kill are free. And if one of them gets arrested, he goes to prison for a while and in a month you see him on the streets again.

God, why?

Also, it's really sad when the same system which gives you the opportunity to succeed now comes whenever it likes, takes everything from you and finally puts you in prison. This system can take everything from you without having to prove anything.

In all the things I went through I never heard an honest word. All the things people said about me were lies. Nobody had the strength or compassion to stop them. In the past, people would say: "Every suspect is considered innocent until they are proven guilty in a court of law." Nowadays we are considered guilty until we prove ourselves innocent.

Where is the America we were dreaming of? Where is the country we were bragging about? Where are the good old days? We will always remember the good old days when America had a voice and the whole world respected our country. Our politicians are 'deaf.' They don't care, don't hear, and don't see. The whole world is against us. They don't listen to the world; don't even listen to the American people, even if 65 percent disagree with their policies. The American people don't trust them anymore. They are right not to trust them because they fool people all the time. Everything has become a business. The new motto is "your misfortune is my gain" and prisons become more crowded by the day.

One out of nine Americans has been to prison or is now in prison. And when somebody gets released from prison, they are condemned for life because they are labeled as felons and cannot find a job.

When people hear the word 'felony,' they get scared. Some people are afraid that they might get arrested just for talking with you and others think of you as a dangerous person. As a result, after a couple of years, some of the former prisoners end up going back to prison. I believe that after you've been convicted of something that is not a serious crime and after you've been to prison and been punished for what you've done, you should have the chance to return to life with all of your rights and not be labeled as a felon forever. People should have the right to live free and to enjoy their life once again.

I don't believe people should go to prison the first time they make a mistake or a slip-up. They should get probation first and not convicted as a felon because with a felony they can be sent to prison at anytime.

For example, if you are in a friend's car and he gets stopped by the police and they find a gun, then you are heading to prison for five years. Why? Because you shouldn't be close to a gun! But if somebody rapes an eight year old girl, he'll go to prison for only 18 months!

It sounds unbelievable, but it's true.

I don't know why this system wants us to be second class citizens, why all of our rights are taken away, why, instead of being rescued when we fall, we are pushed even further down? It's so unfair not to have any support from the government. The people who are conscious about what is going on and how unjust the system

72

is can never get high positions in society, and those people who are in high positions either ignore what's going on or just feel comfortable with the whole situation. Who will do something to change what is happening now?

My friends, before I had to pay for such injustice with great pain and heartache, I always believed the police when they charged someone with a crime because I thought they were trustworthy and told the truth. I believed that they protected us and I didn't even care to hear the other side. I told myself, "The police charged them so that means they must be guilty."

How naive was I and how guilty I felt when I got out of jail and went back home. Whenever I turned on the TV, on the news they were talking about my son and me. From all the things they said not even one word was true. So now, whenever I see somebody being charged with a crime, I believe nothing. I start thinking that he is finished, because I know that he cannot defend himself.

This terrible thing has to stop. This is very difficult though, because there are so many vital interests. That's why they hide the truth from people. Among us there are traitors and traps everywhere. Any little thing you do might land you in prison.

I want you to know that this angel of death, the FBI, The Grim Reaper, has no soul and no heart. When it shows up, it leaves behind ruins. Regardless if you are big or small, blind or lame, disabled or even sick, this system can imprison you. The goal is to destroy you. That's why it's like cancer: it works secretly. The only thing you are allowed to do is call a lawyer. They are aware of that, though when the lawyer comes, the first thing he'll do is to tell you to bring him $20,000 to start your case. And here's the important question, how could you find $20,000 in one day? So you are destined to lose.

In prison I was told that the sentencing guidelines were unconstitutional, that's why they threw them out after thirty years. Now judges can do whatever they like, which means that they are allowed to sentence you to as many years as they like. I'm not sure if it's better to be judged by judges who can sentence you to countless years of imprisonment. And when you have judges that compete with each other on who will give longer sentences before they retire, you can only imagine what is going to happen to you if your destiny is in their hands.

In any case, when I was brought to court, I was sentenced according to the guidelines, but if the judge was allowed and had the chance to decide on his own, he would never have sent me to prison. The first judge who gave me 'probation' was a really just judge. I truly wish him to be blessed in his life. He rescued me.

One of the prisoners told me that he was sentenced to five years in prison by a judge, but if he went by the 'guidelines,' he would have only received probation. The big problem though isn't this, it's something else. The government has to prevent the authorities from falsely charging people and stop them from destroying innocent people just because they want to put them in prison as it happened in my case. They don't charge people only for the offense they've committed, but they also charge them with five to ten more false charges!

Not one prisoner I've talked with has said that he was accused only for the offense they had committed. They were all charged with a lot more false charges. I cannot understand why they show so much careless hostility.

Figure 18 - The Author and his son

We, the American citizens, give our country everything, even our own blood when we are asked to do so. Therefore the country should love and be fair to its citizens.

I cannot even begin to speak about the things I've seen. I saw dark souls, dark hearts, lies and hypocrisy, a society totally unjust and corrupted. Not only is this *status quo* to blame, but it is also unfair and most importantly, cruel!

My friends, prison has become our 'second home.' Like in Greece, when in the 1960's every house had an immigrant, now in America something similar happens or even worse. More or less, nowadays, there's no home that doesn't have someone in prison.

The system functions in such a way that you cannot survive if you don't betray somebody. Ninety-five percent of the people do whatever they are told to do to save themselves. As a result, your dignity is stripped and you are ridiculed in your community. And then maybe they will reduce your prison sentence by a couple of years. Or they might do away with your sentence altogether just because they can do whatever they want.

When my lawyers asked me if I wanted to cooperate with the authorities and they might help me, I didn't understand the question completely and I said "yes" because I had nothing to hide. Afterwards they explained to me what they wanted me to do, basically, is to rat other people out. Then I replied, "The worst person of the people I know and hang out with is way better than me." I told them the truth and I promised to reply with honesty to all of their questions. They congratulated me and said that I was doing the right thing.

My friends, every single human, in order to succeed in their lives, must have goals and targets and they have to believe in them. Faith is the miraculous power that has a huge impact on the psychological condition of a human, on their career, and their general progress.

Figure 19 - With Family and Friends

The principles of life were created in a similar way, like religion, science and all the cultural values. Let's stop here to admire the power of faith upon all its expressions and first of all upon religion. When faith is strong, then a human becomes an unstoppable giant. The influence of having faith in science created today's miracle of scientific progress and the evolution of human life. We all know that throughout history great scholars and scientists were pursued and brought to trial only because they believed in something that went against the *status quo* of their times.

For example, Galileo said that the earth goes around the sun. When he was persecuted by his peers and tried for heresy by the Roman Inquisition, he had only one option to avoid the death penalty: to recant what he had said. In court he recanted, but once he was released and cleared of any offense, he said "it goes around indeed!" *It might be noted here that he was then tried again by The Inquisition, convicted of heresy, and spent the rest of his life in prison for his beliefs.* The same happens with moral and cultural values. This is the same faith that makes heroes fight for their homeland and their freedom. That same faith pushed forward Greek heroes for their Independence in 1821 to distinguish themselves in glory and immortality and the same faith urged the martyrs of the Church to sacrifice everything for their beliefs.

So if we don't believe in what we want to achieve in life, how is it possible to accomplish it without the influence of faith? A man cannot live without faith. If we really believe in a better tomorrow then we should fight for it, for our children, for our grandchildren, so that future generations might be grateful to us. We need to do something. We need to convince our politicians, people with authority in any government, of any church, and of any organization, that they should declare fearlessly: "no more innocent people in prison and stop the hypocrisy."

I assume that good people are everywhere and that they will do something to restore justice in America. They might change the laws and judge people with existing concrete evidence and not on false witnesses and accusations. It's very sad to hear Americans saying they will go to Canada or Mexico when they get out of prison so they can die free. Every time I hear on TV the phrases "Family Values" and "Homeland Security," I get disgusted.

Why do the people who claim this destroy people and ruin families every day?

They send fathers and mothers to prison and leave children on the streets totally unprotected and helpless. If those kids are fortunate enough, they might have grandfathers and grandmothers to take care of them and to raise them with their small retirement funds. Over sixty percent of children in America grow up without their parents. Many prisoners tell me that their wives are also in prison and they don't even know where their children are. Is it not enough to put one parent in prison? Obviously the system doesn't care.

Non-citizens in America who have lived in the USA their entire life with their families and who only have a green card have it even worse. Once they serve their sentence in prison they are deported to their homelands immediately. They'll never come back to America and will never see their children again. The green card just gives you the right to stay in America temporarily and the government can take it back whenever it wants. That's why it's very important for somebody to become an

American citizen. Personally, if I hadn't secured my citizenship before my arrest, they would have sent me back to Greece forever.

What is the meaning of "Homeland Security?" I don't believe America is in danger by any external threat. I believe that all this is just an excuse for them to pass laws against our freedom and treat us with no mercy. In 1940 Mussolini sank Italian ships by his order and then blamed it on the Greeks so he could have an excuse and his people's support to attack Greece.

I think that this same policy continues today. Our politicians have taken everything they wanted from the American people. We were told that Bin Laden knocked down our buildings, so we should go to Afghanistan and attack him. We were told that Saddam Hussein has nuclear bombs, so we had to attack him before he attacks us. Our military forces did their duty with honor and effectiveness. Now it is time for our politicians to do their part. Personally, I'm against war and in support of peace.

During peaceful times children bury their parents, but during war, parents bury their children.

War is the science of destruction.

Figure 20 - The Author with his son

Today is October 19, 2005, and the whole day I've been listening to the news about Saddam Hussein's trial. Many journalists ask several people if the court in Iraq will be fair. I wonder if they are just paid to ask such ridiculous questions. Is it possible for a judge who is a criminal himself to be just? Of course not. All of them, more or less, have stained their hands with the blood of innocent people. However, I don't care about what they do in Iraq and Afghanistan. I do care about what they do in my home in America. I want to challenge those journalists to tell me if their child goes to court in the United States, do they believe that the court will be just?

My friends, from the things you hear, believe nothing and from what you see believe only half of it. In any case, whenever we realize that we are in danger from a foreign country, we'll shed our blood for the country we've loved and still love so much. Yet, we should tell people the truth. Only then will people unite.

I respect our politicians very much because I think that they succeeded not by chance, but because they deserved it. Now I want to tell them that when people are united, they are unbeatable. I want to tell them that, like the Greek song says, *"Nobody is born to be a murderer,"* and this fake world throws young men in prison. This system is to blame but nobody has brought it to trial. Martha Stewart's imprisonment says a lot: they put her in prison because she sold her shares. Instead of fining her a couple of million dollars in order to help some poor people, they put her in prison. The prisons are full with people like Martha Stewart.

My friends, thirty new prisons and only one University were built in California in the last 20 years. Over 200 large corporations have signed contracts with the prisons for about 15 to 20 years to produce all of their products using cheap prison labor. A laborer who works in a company needs to be paid 20 to 30 dollars per hour, but the prisoners are treated as if they were slaves and get paid 8 to 50 cents per hour.

So, if these companies want contracts to last, they need to have a certain number of employees. That's why they sentence people to 15 to 20 years in prison for the slightest things. That's why the district attorney fights hard in court and tries with thousands of lies to exaggerate and to convict someone for as many years as they can. Their best day is when they send somebody to prison for many years.

Once upon a time in a prison cell a new prisoner arrived. "For how many years are you sentenced?" an old prisoner asked the new one, and the new one replied "ten." "What did you do?" asked the old prisoner. "Nothing" said the new one. "That's impossible," says the old prisoner. "You must've done something, because for doing nothing they sentence you to five years."

In order to get a job in the UNICOR (the factory of the prison) you have to be sentenced for more than five years, or you are not allowed to work there. They give you other duties and they pay you eight cents per hour.

The benefits they get from the prisoners are substantial and it's easy to understand why. Imagine if you had a store with unpaid employees and you gave them only three pieces of clothing per year, second hand, and you fed them what society throws away and if you also gave them one bottle of Coca-Cola per year, you can imagine how much profit you would make. I'm sure you would never choose to close this store.

The telecommunication companies charge us 23 cents per minute, but they earned, just in the last year, 1.5 billion dollars and they donated 40 percent of that to the prisons. I've read many times that each prisoner costs 25,000 dollars per year. If it costs that much, why do the police need to bring false charges against you? They should just arrest the real criminals.

My friends, all of you who raise your children with so much effort, think of your anguish and intense desire to see them grow up. And when they become 20 years old, the police will mislead them to do something illegal, like they did to my own child. What will you do then? When your child is exploited, the only solution will be to accept a plea deal about crimes which your child has never actually committed. Then it will be too late and you'll be trying desperately to find an explanation like I did.

The 25,000 dollars each prisoner costs the government, like they say, is perhaps an excuse that they use to take more taxes. Except the government gives this money to the prisons and they waste it. The only thing I know is that they try as hard as they can to keep you in prison for a long time. This says a lot. If they like, according to the law, they can give you six months in a Half-Way House and six months of House Arrest but they give you three months grudgingly and for the slightest infraction, they can cut that off too.

So, we shouldn't expect any kind of help from the prison system. I never heard one word about the profit companies make off this prison labor. Over 150 prisons are controlled by individuals. To make a long story short, I see many people investing their money in prisons which means that they invest their money in prisoners' lives. That's why I don't see better days. Our children's future is dark. The good people will always hurt and suffer.

If someone wants to govern people, they first have to love them. Only in this way will they protect them. This is something that doesn't exist nowadays.

We hope that someday politicians will start loving their citizens. And if they cannot do this, at least I hope they'll stop destroying them. I hope they will let them live. People have many problems these days and hopefully they do not add more like they did in my case.

Millions of people suffer in prisons without being guilty and they are desperate for help. I make an appeal to all the men and women in power to help people who are suffering; to protect their freedoms and rights; to make our legal system just and trustworthy so that it will stand behind its citizens and not against them. This will make them proud of their country and they'll stick together. Nobody asks for freedom if they commit a crime. What they ask for is the truth, not lies. What I ask from them is not to hold a gun to our head and then ask you if you've committed a crime. Then, you'll have to reply "yes," because if you say "no," they'll pull the trigger, metaphorically speaking.

Figure 21 - With my son and special friend, Irini Politis

Nowadays they don't judge depending on evidence but by their power. I appeal to them to give a chance to those who, unwillingly, made a mistake in their life. I beg them to give those people back their rights so that they might live a better life and offer their country as much as they can. In Beeville, Texas, the population is 20,000 and 7,000 of them are in prison. How is this possible in our days? I read in a newspaper that in Amsterdam, Holland, only 75 people are in prison. I guess all the angels live there and all the criminals live in America, which is obviously not true.

My friends, it is twice as painful when I think that all this damage done to me was caused by Greeks from the beginning to the end. I still cannot understand why. Greeks against Greeks in a foreign country! Even when I die I still won't believe it. I was proud of being Greek but now I'm not sure anymore. If those two Greeks of the FBI had done their job the way they were supposed to, I would shake their hands. What they did though, was mislead 22 innocent people and ruin 22 families. It's a shame. If I was them, I wouldn't be able to sleep at night having that on my conscience. I'll never forgive them for the damage, the pain, and the grief they caused us. I'm being truthful; I still have no clue why I am in prison.

That's why we need to fight for a just society and the law has to punish real criminals, not innocent people. The only way for somebody to prevent injustice is jury duty. Many people believe that it's a waste of time when they are called to judge someone. I had the same impression whenever I was called and I never went because I couldn't understand the English language well enough to serve. This is the only way we have, as citizens, to defend justice when somebody is on trial. Those people should realize what a huge responsibility they have when a human life depends on their decision. Life or death of the accused depends on them. That's why they should be very careful when they judge someone. They need not be misled by someone's lies or false oaths. Everybody there swears to tell the truth, but they don't. The jury must listen to all sides of the case and not only one. They need to judge based on concrete evidence. The witnesses who testify against someone might be biased and ignore the well-being of the accused. The district attorney has the power to charge you no matter who you are. I pray that God will guide jurors to reach a decision that is just so they can save lives. I want you to keep in mind that 93 percent of defendants accept a plea bargain from the government and only seven percent go to trial. Only three percent of those who go to trial might not be convicted, but the other 97 percent will all be convicted.

My friends, I do not wish my situation on anyone. I feel like someone who has died but can still see and hear. I want you to know that if something bad happens to you, all your friends will abandon you and forget you. Very few people will stand by your side. It is then that you will distinguish the real humans, the real friends, those who really love you. I've never learned so much in my whole lifetime than I did from 2002 until 2006. I'm not sure about life after death but I do know that in this life there's a heaven and a hell. And hell is separated from heaven only by a few feet and a fence. When you lose your freedom, you've lost everything. Nothing is the same anymore. The sun doesn't shine and the flowers don't bloom. Everything around you takes on a gloomy shadow of pain and the mournful sight of death. Even the grass on the outside of the fence looks more green and beautiful when you see it through the eyes of a prisoner.

The greatest day of my life will be on April 17, 2006, when I'll return to life and head back home to the people I love. I'll go back to those who loved me and experienced my sorrow with me. The only thing that gives me hope is the thought that there are people who love me, think of me, and wait for me. I feel grateful to the people who helped me and kept me alive. I will always be thankful for them and I'll always owe them my gratitude. I thank them all from the bottom of my heart and promise to stand by their side under any circumstances in grief or in happiness.

One night somebody dreamt that he was walking on the seashore with God. He saw two pairs of footprints in the sand, one pair that belonged to him and the other one to God. Finally, when he looked behind him, he saw that many times in his path there was only one pair of footprints in his most troubling times. This saddened him and he asked, "Almighty God, I just saw that in the hardest times of my life there is only one set of footprints. Why, when I needed you the most, did you abandon me?"

And God answered him: "My precious child, I love you and I never left or forsook you. During your times of trial and pain, you saw only one pair of footprints because that's when I carried you."

The same with me. You may not see me, but that's because I carry you close to my heart. I wish happiness to those who were not willing to stand by me and who were glad this happened to me even though I was always generous to them. I truly don't know why this happens. When someone suffers, other people are happy, and when someone is happy the others are unhappy. It's very sad and I want to make them aware of something because they pretend to be good Christians.

Jesus taught that we should love our neighbor as we love ourselves and if they are suffering, hungry or in prison, we should help them. My advice is this: if you love someone, show them now and don't keep it a secret. Nobody knows what you feel inside. Spend your time with the people you love.

There's nothing more painful than the despair of a person who considers themselves dead, like I feel now. My friends, we live in a corrupted society and it will continue to make people suffer if we do not speak out on this injustice.

The System is Responsible

On the morning of December 4, 2002, like every other day, I went to work at 7 am. I worked the whole day and in the evening I went to the kafenió I was renting with my son. About 8 pm, after no customers had come and it was icing outside, we closed up shop and went back home. Everything was great, as usual.

I went home and slept. In my sleep I dreamt that I was at the fountain of the village where I grew up. Then I started to walk away from the village. A voice told me not to leave but when I turned around to go back, I suddenly appeared in the Garden of Eden. It was full of beautiful trees and many flowers. At the side of this garden there was a big apple tree with many beautiful apples. I was wondering when and how all these grew so fast and then one of the villagers said, "You've been away from the village for a long time."

On December 5, 2002, at 7 am my wife woke me up. She looked kinda scared and said, "Something bad is gonna happen to us. When our kids wake up, tell them to be careful and to stay home all day." I said "What is it? What are you talking about?" She replied, "It's raining ice outside and one of the trees behind our home fell down."

I felt a bit scared but I wanted to encourage her and said to her: "Where did you want the tree to fall? Not up, of course?" Instead of laughing, she said "Something bad is going to happen."

I fell asleep for a while and about 9 am I heard a huge noise and different voices at the door. I jumped out of my bed; I went to the bathroom and looked out of the window. I saw 5 or 6 men walking up and down in my back yard. I thought a gas pipe had broken from the ice.

Before I gave it a second thought they pushed in the door and came in. They put a gun to my head, handcuffed me and pulled me outside.

"Please let me get dressed," I said. I put on my

clothes with difficulty and with fear that they might pull the trigger. In the hallway I saw my son standing up and having his hands in handcuffs against the wall. "What's going on"? I asked him. "I don't know, Dad," he said. "Do whatever you're told to do," I said, "and be strong."

When they took me out of my house, I saw over 10 police cars. When a neighbor asked them what's going on, they asked him if he had watched the movie *Godfather*. They kept my wife, my father and my other son captives on the couch for 4 hours. They couldn't move from there. If somebody wanted to go to the bathroom, the police escorted them with guns in their hands.

For four hours they turned my house into their office. They looked everywhere, loaded everything they wanted and left a paper about the stuff they had picked up, as if they had to answer to anyone. They forced me to get in one of their cars and we left. We passed my restaurant and my kafenió, picked up the keys and then they led me directly to jail. On our way, they supposedly read me my rights and then said, "We'll ask you some questions and if you like, you can answer them."

I told them the truth about everything they asked me. I had nothing to hide. I only asked them to allow me to have my arms handcuffed in front of me because they were hurting behind me. They responded by saying I was a criminal and they would treat me the way I was supposed to be treated. Afterwards they led me to their headquarters.

They processed me, took my picture and fingerprints, and then led me to an office, where they interrogated me. After I had told them the whole truth, they wanted me to tell them that I have two million dollars and demanded me to confess where I had this money hidden. This was the amount they claimed I earned from the kafenió. Also they wanted me to tell them about other people, if I knew anything. I told them that the people I hung out with and who used to come to my kafenió were very good people. "Even the worst of them is better than me," I said. Then I was told that my son is in the next room, that he burst into tears and has started confessing everything. I told them, "Didn't I tell you that my son is a good boy and he'll tell you the truth about anything you'll ask him?"

They thought I was being sarcastic and exclaimed: "You don't want to cooperate with us and your choices will destroy your son."

"Do your job the best way you can," I said.

After that, around 5 pm and after a long hardship, I was led to jail. I started there all over again, from the basement, the photos, the finger prints and, finally from floor to floor until I reached the 3rd floor. There I was given a blue ribbon around my wrist with my name and number on it. I was also told that I was allowed to call my home if I wanted to. Indeed I called my home and when my other son answered the phone, one of the guards shouted at me to hang up.

I didn't understand that he was talking to me

though. So he came close to me, took the phone from my hand and exclaimed, "Don't you know that you don't have any rights now that you're a prisoner?" I apologized for not hearing him and he said, "Next time you better hear me."

Then he took me and locked me in a jail cell. All the other inmates were together outside of the cells, but I was inside. Around 9 pm he took me out of the cell. Then I saw a Greek woman I used to know, sitting in a corner, in chains. In the beginning I couldn't believe that it was her. I thought I was hallucinating. When I asked her why she was there, she said that they accused her of being a card dealer in my kafenió! I almost lost my mind because this woman had never been at the kafenió. The next day they realized their fault and, after giving her a paper to sign that she wouldn't sue them, she went back home.

Around 10 pm they took my clothes and told me to take a cold shower with ten more people.

Afterwards I put on their orange uniform and they handed me a plastic basket with all of my belongings in it: half of a blanket, a small towel, a tooth brush, soap and a comb. Then we took the elevator and they guided me to the 4th floor. I passed two iron doors which opened automatically from the inside. They put me in jail cell no 26.

When they shut the door of my cell I felt incredibly cold, I thought that my life was ending. I started thinking of my son, about how he could endure all this. They put him somewhere else, so that the knife would go deeper in the wound. I started looking around at the four walls, the toilet-seat on the concrete floor with a small faucet above it, and the small iron bed without a mattress. I pressed a button which was next to the door and somebody answered. I asked him for a mattress, because it was freezing cold and he said: "When I have one, I'll give you one." I waited until 2 am and nobody showed up. I laid the towel down in the corner of the cell on the cold concrete. Then I tried to cover myself up with the small blanket. I stayed alive with the warmth of my breath that night. At 4 am they led us all out of the jail cells, to give us what they call "breakfast." They gave us rice and beans and two slices of bread on a plastic plate.

I was shivering from the cold and I gave my food to someone else who was really hungry. To be honest I ate nothing for 6 days. The only thing I wanted was water. I felt no hunger at all. The 6th day, a black guy felt sorry for me and once we got out of the jail cells, he handed me a plastic cup with soup. He had added some hot running water to soften it and told me to eat it. Then he gave me an undershirt, I wore it and survived the next few days thanks to him. The next day, December 11, 2002, it was freezing cold. At 4 am I was led to the basement and locked in a jail cell until 9 am. Then I went to another place to get prepared for court. It was there that I first saw my son. Actually, they shackled us in chains. My ankle was shackled to my son's ankle. Ankle to ankle we walked slowly to the police van.

It was freezing in the van. As we arrived at the court building, they placed us in a room for about an hour. Then they came and took the handcuffs off and led us to the courtroom with our ankles in chains.

Figure 22 - With my son and two cousins

My lawyer had advised me not to look at or greet anyone, because it was prohibited. When I entered the courtroom and saw the place crowded, I felt relieved. I wouldn't change that moment and the solace I felt from my people for all the gold in the world. I raised my hands up and sent them kisses. Then one of the guards pushed me to keep walking and I ignored him. That moment I felt as if I were in the arms of all the people there. Then they started the bond hearing which I'll never forget.

I was sitting with my son, between our lawyers. On one side there was Mr. Nixon and on the other side Mr. Plumides. The district attorney who was on the far side was using his wrath and lies to convince the judge that my son and I were dangerous for society and that we should remain in jail. He said that if we got out we might escape to Greece. Afterwards it was our lawyers' turn to speak. They fought hard for our freedom. The judge then read the charges into the record and if we were found guilty of all the charges against us, we would be sentenced up to180 years in prison. Finally the judge decided to free us on bond, I couldn't understand how all this was happening to us. The only thing I understood was that we were in a lot of trouble and I didn't know how the story would end.

Then they escorted us back to the van and we returned to jail. When I arrived, some of the inmates were awaiting the news. When I told them that we got bond, they were very happy for me. Around 6 pm I was called to go downstairs.

They gave me my clothes; I put them on and left the jail. When I saw my people, I fell into their arms and felt so much warmth. I went back home and my relatives and friends were there, waiting for me. It was a huge celebration and an unforgettable moment.

It was a miracle that I got out of prison at all because this gave me the chance to put my affairs in order. If I hadn't gotten out that day, things would have become very difficult for my family and me.

My son, Gus, was still in jail, because they wanted to find a GPS device for his ankle. They would put the device on his ankle in order to have him under constant observation. On Friday, a man came over to check our house and my other son, Vasili, pled with him to bring my son back home that night. If he didn't come home that night, he would have to stay in jail until Monday. The man said that it wasn't up to him and he left without giving us any promises. Finally at 6 pm somebody rang the bell. We rushed out and saw this man who had my son with him. I wish this man all the blessings in the world because he gave us such a great joy that evening.

Fear lurked everywhere though. In our home we talked quietly in the dark, because we thought they might have put cameras in the house. When I turned on the TV, I was the first story on the news. My restaurant was shown and there were random pictures of me with wrestlers, pictures of me in Greece and false stories. In the morning we went to work and we had no idea if we would come back at night or if they would put us in jail again. My lawyer told me that the district attorney was trying to revoke our bond. He appealed our bond and fortunately it was denied or else we would go back to jail.

When we calmed down a bit, I went to the bank to withdraw some money.

I had in my account about $80,000 to pay my lawyers. When I entered the bank, everybody hid behind their desks and they were looking at me like I came from Mars. I finally went to a cashier I knew for years to ask for my money. She said that all of my accounts, including my restaurant account, were frozen by the government and there was nothing they could do. Then the real trouble started.

When I went to the restaurant, all the representatives from the companies which supplied us with food and the owner of the building had left urgent messages for me. They were all waiting for me in order to get paid because all my business checks had bounced. And on top of all that, the whole week I was in jail my business partner deposited all the collections of the restaurant in those frozen accounts. The money could be deposited but not withdrawn. Not even one dollar was in our pockets. My brothers had given all of their money to my lawyers. It was Christmas time when I started looking for some help. All people were decorating their houses and were preparing for the holidays.

It was then that I remembered my father. When I was a little boy, he used to give me some advice. He told me that wherever I go to "open a new house." And when I asked him where I could find the money to do so, he explained that what he meant was to make a new friend. This is what I did, wherever I went, I made friends, and I always had friends, this was my reward. But in this difficult moment, most of them betrayed me. I screwed up, like the Greek hero Athanasios Diakos. When all of his soldiers abandoned him, he saw close to him his servant named Bisbirikos.

"What are you doing here, Bisbirikos?" Diakos asked him. "They'll kill you. Go away and save yourself like the others did." And his servant replied, "No way captain, I'm not going anywhere without you. I'll stay here and die with you."

Then Diakos shook his head and said, "If I only had more men like you, I would ask for nothing more!"

I am proud to say though that not all of my friends abandoned me. In my entire life I never refused to help others, people or organizations or churches. None of these people, organizations, or churches went to the trouble of making one phone call to my suffering home, which was in the dark at the time. No words of comfort which we so desperately needed. I always treated others the same way I would want them to treat me. I was always very generous. That's why somebody from above sent me a few people to give me a hand.

One day I was in the restaurant and a Greek man came in. He said, "Will you make me a cup of coffee? I came to see how you're doing."

We sat down to drink our coffee.

"Do you remember me?" he asked.

I said "of course" and then he said, "Do you remember that in 1986 I came and asked you for a job and your fellow partner told me that there's no job available. Then I told you that I had three children to support and no money to feed them. You gave me $200 and promised to give me a job in a couple of days." This had happened indeed.

I said, "I barely remember this, but why are you telling me this now?"

"I have $30,000 and I will give it to you,"

Instead of saying "thank you," I burst into tears.

Some other people also offered me help and I wish all of them the best. But at that moment, when I was facing 180 years of imprisonment, all I wanted was the support of my friends, not the money. Of course I needed the money, but I knew that I would have to sell the fruit of my life's work in order to pay off my debts. The people's support, their love, and their concern for me and my son, gave me the courage to stand up in court. This made me feel that I wasn't alone. Even our enemies changed their minds, when they saw this huge outpouring of support. They tried to say that there were as many people at my hearing as there were at John Gotti's trial."

The pain and the concern on my family's and friends' faces said a lot. All those people came to court to support us. They didn't come for the sake of appearance. I was told that some of my "friends" were happy to see me suffer.

"What happened to our friend with the successful life?" they said.

Never mind. I'm sure that I've been generous to them sometime in their life.

My friends please give your support to people who really need it, not to charities for fame.

We spent Christmas together and right when I got ready to put the issues in order and to heal some of the wounds, another disaster struck.

On January 3rd of 2003, I was working in my restaurant and the telephone rang. I answered and a strange voice said, "We'll be there in 5 minutes. Don't go any-where." I got scared. I felt my blood rushing to my head. There was something in me saying that they would put me in jail again. I called my lawyer and informed him about the phone call. I told him that I got scared and that, in my opinion, it was the FBI. Then he said, "They can do nothing to you, because you have a lawyer. Don't speak a word."

After a while, two FBI agents came in as if they were about to catch the notorious gangster Katsantonis. When they ordered me to go outside, I then realized that something was going on and started trembling. When I got out, they handcuffed me and said, "You are under ar-rest because you threatened one of our witnesses."

Honestly, my prayer at that moment was: "Please God, take me now, I want to die, I don't want to live any more. I can't stand this anymore."

"All people die once on this earth, but me, the unprivileged one, dies every day....," like the Greek song says.

I gave the little money I had in my pocket to the cashier and told her to call my home and tell them the bad news.

With much difficulty I walked to their car. My strength was fading away, I couldn't walk. They led me back to jail and everything started all over again. After 5 hours of hardship, they brought me back to the jail cell. I was exhausted. I thought that they had decided to destroy us and I felt they would never leave us alone. The next day I called my lawyer and he said, "If they arrest you a second time, there is only a one in a hundred chance you will get out. We'll go to court again next week and maybe you'll make it and get out."

That day came and we went to court

There they said that I had threatened one of their witnesses, that I had talked to somebody I shouldn't talk to, and that I tried to communicate with another witness by computer.

Figure 23 - The Author with his two sons, his wife and sister and brother with his little son

When I first got out of jail, the FBI made one of my friends call me. When I picked up the phone, he said that he was close to my restaurant and wanted to come over and see me. I said, "I'd love to see you, but you are in the same trouble as I am. My lawyer has advised us not to talk to each other but some day, when this is over, we can talk again,"

I hung up the phone and 15 minutes later he

119

showed up at the restaurant. I had the feeling that something was wrong, but I wasn't sure. When I went to his table and greeted him he started right away telling lies about the case, stuff that the Feds told him to say. I guess he was worried that he might forget his words or that a wire from the device he wore might get disconnected and he would be exposed. He said, "Did you see what your son has done to us by paying a cop for protection?"

Such a thing had never happened and he knew that. But the FBI wanted to have some evidence against me just in case we went to trial because they had no evidence against me.

I realized that he was sent by "them" and I asked him why he was in such a hurry. He gave me no answer but only looked away. I advised him that he should not talk to me or my son. Then I left his table.

One other day I went with some friends to a Greek restaurant to eat. The owner's son was in the same case as us. I had known them for many years and we had worked together. We ate and before I left I wished them 'good luck' for their son.

Right afterwards they called the FBI and said that I went there and threatened them. I guess their son had cooperated with the FBI. They preferred to crucify me and my son by telling lies, in order to avoid prison. As far as their third argument, another lie, because I never even had a computer.

My other son, Vasili, proved with witnesses in court that all these accusations were lies. And when the judge heard all this, he turned to the district attorney and told him, "I can't keep this man in prison for no reason. Don't bother him again unless his case comes through me." The judge scolded them on this because they tried to go over him by appealing to a different judge who gave them permission to arrest me again.

The same night I went back home. The next day I started again going around trying to borrow money. The lawyers were asking for money and they were very expensive. When I had paid them all and tried to take a breath, my lawyer said that we should find yet another lawyer, who was a specialist in opening my checking account in the bank. Again, I went around borrowing money and after I had paid him, my lawyer said, "Now you should hire another lawyer from Washington DC, Mr. Plato Cacheris." Plato was a great lawyer, but he wanted $50,000 in order to help me. I went to an uncle of mine and, with tears in my eyes, I begged him to lend me this money, so that I could send it right away. He went to the bank and took out a loan against his house. He gave me the money and I sent it to the Washington lawyer immediately.

Of course, I don't have any complaints towards my lawyers. I believe they tried their best. The only thing is that they were very expensive for me!

At the end, after four months of huge worries and hardships, in April of 2003, my lawyers invited me to their office. Together, all of them assured me that they had achieved the best plea agreement they could and that they had only two hours to answer the district attorney if I agree to it.

If I said 'no,' the FBI warned that they'd put all of my family in jail. And, they added, this was a promise not a threat. Mr. Plato assured me that the fact that they had said this to him showed that they were serious about it.

Then I asked them about the deal. I had to pay a $350,000 penalty and go to prison for 33 to 42 months with my son as a package deal.

I asked them if there was a better option and they all said "no." Then they said that all the other defendants who were charged had already cooperated with the district attorney and they would be used as witnesses against us, if we went to trial. They would testify to the lies they would be given. Under those circumstances, my only choice was to accept the plea. Another problem was that we were two people involved in the case and if I won, maybe my son would go to prison for many years.

When I heard two and a half years imprisonment,

this made my blood run cold and I started trembling again. The time had come for me to plead to a false charge for something I hadn't committed, "Racketeering." As far as the financial penalty, this didn't cause me any worry. If I had to sell my business to pay them, I would accept this as a discipline from God. The Apostle Paul said: *"God disciplines those He loves with sorrow."* If this is correct, then I'll admit that the Lord gave me everything I had and the Lord took it away. Finally, I stayed in their office speechless with my head bowed for a long time. Then Mr. Plato told me not to be sad because he said he would arrange it so that I could go to the same prison as my son. Then I accepted the plea and left.

When I got out of the building, it was evening time and everything around me seemed fake and dark. When I got back home, my family was waiting for the news. I told them everything and that we should adjust ourselves to this, that the pathway of our torment would be a long one. After about a month, we went to court, in front of the judge, to sign the plea agreement.

My lawyer told me that I had to swear under oath that I had committed the offense I was charged with. In other words I would swear and admit to something I had never committed. If I didn't swear though, the judge would never accept the plea deal. Thus, since the whole case was full of lies, I became a liar to save myself. From all the things that my lawyers promised me, the only things that were true were the punishment and the fine. My son and I did not go to the same prison and no lawyer asked about me after that. I sent them letters from prison and they never replied.

When we made the agreement, they asked me when I could pay the fine. Without being aware of the problems I would have to deal with, I said that I would pay them before we went to court. I had the impression that things would be like they were before they arrested me. The problem was that everywhere I went to borrow money, although before all this they would lend me money, everyone declined me.

Time was passing by and there was nothing I could do. My lawyer said if I didn't pay them before my court date, chances were they would take my shopping center and sell it off by auction to get their money. Plus this would look bad to the court and they might give me a heavier sentence of 42 months instead of 33. It was really important for me to keep my word. Besides that, if I lost my entire shopping center, I would also lose my house and I would still be in debt over $200,000.

Figure 24 - With Family

Ten months passed with this agony! Just as my hopes started turning into despair and my pain into a storm, somebody from above again sent me a really good person. This man wanted us to become partners in my shopping center and he would give me the half of my shopping center's value. I showed him the contract that proved its value and he agreed to the purchase.

"Next week we can sign the papers," he said.

The value of my shopping center was $1.6 million

and I owed $600,000 to the bank. The agreement was that he would give me $500,000 cash and pay off the additional $600,000 loan, because this was exactly the amount of money I needed to pay the fine and lawyers. So I called my lawyer and told him:

"I want you to make two different contracts for two different buyers." I said this because there was another person who wanted to buy half of my shopping center for $200,000 less than the true value of the shopping center. I didn't have any other choice because I had already received a letter that on December 1, of 2003, I would go to court for sentencing. So I tried to salvage as much as I could.

At 11 am I was planning to sign the contract with the man who offered me $500,000 and, if something bad happened, I would sign with the second man who offered $300,000.

When that day came, I left my home at 4 am. How could I sleep when that day marked a crucial point in my life and my family's future? My mind was full of worries.

I went to the restaurant and waited for 7 am to come. Afterwards I left the restaurant and went to the building where my lawyer's office was. On the 1st floor below his office there was a small restaurant. I had a coffee there and I was thinking: "God, please, don't let my cell phone ring because it might bring me bad news.

At that time, I was used to hearing bad news every time my cell phone rang. At 8 am my cell phone rang and my blood pressure suddenly went up. I thought "my last hope is over. . ." My lawyer was on the phone.

Good morning Mr. Dimitris," he said. "You can come one hour earlier to my office. This man confirmed that he will be here at 9."

This was the only happiness I felt the last 10 months. Everything around me changed, I saw a light of hope and salvation. Then I told him with a faint voice: "I've been here, downstairs, since 7 am. I'm coming up." I went to his office and I hugged him. He asked me if I'm ok. "Now I'm fine," I said.

After a while, the other people came in, we signed the papers, and this man's banker gave my lawyer the check. My lawyer agreed to pay all the people I owed money to.

When everything was done, I thanked them all and then turned to my new partner and said to him that he didn't just make a good purchase, he saved a family.

Finally my lawyer got $10,000 for his job and for me this meant a lot more than money. At least, I had 'pumped the brakes' on my descent. I paid off the money I owed and felt alive again. On December 1st 2003, we went to court with our heads up and with a clean conscience. My sentence would range from 33 months up to 41 months. It was up to the judge to give me as many months as he wished within the guidelines. The district attorney suggested 41 months, the highest penalty. My lawyer, Mr. Plumides, asked the judge to make an exception and to consider me as an example for my dignity and honorable past and to give me 33 months. This made the judge remain silent for about 10 minutes. Then he asked me if I had anything to say. I raised my hands and asked for mercy. Finally he gave me the lowest sentence, 33 months.

Afterwards the district attorney asked the judge to add four more months to my son's sentence, which meant 37 months, due to a speeding ticket. The judge finally tacked on four more months to his sentence. What do you think? Would it be better if he was given four months in prison or if they had taken his driver's license away for a year? Then the judge allowed us to "self-surrender" to prison, which was much better than being taken to prison from the courtroom.

On December 16th 2003, one week before Christmas, everyone was decorating their houses with joy, but we had to take my son to prison.

This black Tuesday morning of December 16th came and I'll never forget it. When my son said 'goodbye' to his friends, his cat, and to all those who were there and when he kissed his mother goodbye, she hugged him and cried out "where are you going, my son?" This had to be the worst moment I had experienced throughout this whole ordeal.

Finally we got in the car and left, because we had to be at the prison's gate before noon. Then a man came, handcuffed his hands and took him away from us as he told us to leave. Then the darkness covered everything.

So we set out on our way back. My sister was speechless and the Greek singer Stelios Kazantzides was singing on the CD player:

> *"Unjust human, why are you like that?*
> *Don't you have any feelings in your soul?*
> *Why did you separate me from my sweet love?*
> *Since I'm not guilty and I've done nothing wrong*
> *Why you made my poor mother cry?*
> *Unjust human, why do you want to see me in prison?*
> *Some day my mother's prayers will set me free.*
> *But her curses will burn you."*

After him Manolis Angelopoulos started singing another song:

"Oh heart, turn into marble, turn into steel,
so that they won't hurt you again,
Since nobody felt for you,
Become strong so that nobody will hurt you again.
Oh my heart, turn into marble and ignore them,
If they want, in private or in public,
to humiliate you."

At the end, we went back home. Our pain was too heavy to carry. Everything around us was talking about our missing son. The next day I wanted to visit prison to see how my son was doing, but I had to have permission from my probation officer. For a whole week I couldn't get in touch with him. When I finally did, he gave me the permission and told me to just leave him a voice mail next time I wanted to visit my son.

I burst into tears and thanked him a lot. I was used to feeling pain and to being treated unfairly, so, whenever somebody showed me mercy, I burst into tears.

Figure 25 - The Author and son with friends

Under those circumstances, we 'celebrated' a black Christmas. After everything was arranged, I was glad that I hadn't lost my house. Apart from that, I was getting prepared to go to prison.

On December 10th of 2003, I received a letter that I needed to report to prison before noon, of February 5, 2004. I was hoping to go where my son was, so that we'd be together. Unfortunately I was sent to another prison,

500 feet away from my son's prison.

When that day came, I woke up at 5 am and got dressed quickly. I said goodbye to everyone. I kissed my other son, who was still in bed and left. My son wanted to wake up and come with me, but I told him to stay. I knew that time was against me and I wanted to avoid feeling more pain. I didn't want to stay home any longer because it just made me feel worse. Just sitting around and thinking about the things that had happened to me made me very sad. So I left with a cousin and a friend of mine and we headed to prison. Honestly, I remember almost nothing from that morning.

At noon we were waiting outside of the prison. I gave my people everything I had with me, because you are not allowed to take personal items with you.

A man from the prison picked me up, handcuffed me and led me to a temporary jail cell. Then my life as a convict began. The hours started becoming days. The days became months and the months became years.

The clock stopped and with it my life stopped as well. Everything now looked forward to April 17th 2006, when my life could once again be continued. Then I could collect the broken pieces of my life and begin again.

The bridge bent but didn't break.

In the beginning I thought about running to avoid prison, but I thought to myself, "My life in prison will be harsh, but being chased by the law, living as a fugitive here and there, would be even harsher..."

My Suffering in Prison

After three hours, a man took me from the jail cell and led me to a room. He told me to take off all of my clothes.   After he checked my mouth, my hair, and my entire body, he gave me a uniform and told me to wear it. Then they sent my original clothes home. They took my fingerprints, pictures, and they gave me a card with my name on it and a number. They told me that I should memorize this number and remember it because I would conduct all prison activities with this number. Of course you have to have some money from the outside, because the only things you are given for free there are a little food and some clothing.

Afterwards they showed me another door in a hallway that I needed to enter. As I entered that door, I found myself in prison. I started looking around to find someone to help me. A prisoner saw me and came close to me.

"Are you new here?" he asked.

"Yes," I answered and he said,

"Go to that room up there to get your clothing."

I went there and I was given all the stuff I would need for my stay there. I was given two blankets, two bed sheets, three pairs of pants, three buttoned down shirts, underwear and shoes and then I was told to go to G2. When I got there, I saw a small bed next to the restrooms.

While I was looking around, another prisoner engaged me: "Why are you looking around? Make your bed quickly before somebody else takes it and you'll have to go to the "hole". You're lucky, because other people come in and they cannot find a bed so they've got to go to the "hole" for 2 to 3 months until a bed opens up.

I thanked him and I made my small bed in my new residence. This is where I would serve my sentence for the next two and a half years.

Everything around me looked gloomy and dark. I heard the flushing of the toilets all night long; the lights were on and people were yelling. It was a real hell. The second night, somebody gave me earplugs to stuff my ears so that I might get some sleep.

The following week, I started the medical exams, shots for this, shots for that.

The third week, they put me in the kitchen to work from 4 am until 12:30 pm and they paid me $7 for the first month.

All this looked to me so ridiculous, cheap and fake. They did everything they could to degrade us. When we got out of the kitchen, they checked us out to see if we had stolen something.

One day they put me in a refrigerator to make some salad and when they left, they locked the door. When I finished my job, I tried to get out but the door was locked. I almost froze to death. After half an hour, someone came over and opened the door. I told him that I suffer from bronchial asthma and when I'm cold I cannot breathe. The next day the same thing happened. The idea of talking to their superior came to mind, but then I thought about the proverb: "a dog doesn't eat another dog".

The entire ordeal was so degrading that I sometimes would go to the bathroom and cry. I said to myself "look at me. How I have sunk so low".

I never wanted the guards to see me like that because it would only make them happy. After a while I realized that the one thing I could control was not to get depressed. Like the song says, *In life's crossroads I cry but nobody can hear me.*

Those first months I suffered greatly. Not even a single hour or a single day passed without me feeling like I had no value.

Easter Sunday came on April 11, 2004.

Five times I went to the telephone to call my family, to give wishes to my wife and son, but my tears caused me to go back to my bed.

I didn't have the courage to talk to them.

Everything in prison is phony. There's no compassion or logic. Anything you ask the guards, you will receive the same answer:"no." Everything functions as if it were a robot. All the guards have become lords of the people who suffer and are prisoners of this system. The people who are in charge there will never help you. Maybe 10 percent of them have some compassion and emotions. In prison you cannot be free. You are allowed to move only for 15 minutes each hour and you always have to be in a certain place at all times. If you are not wherever you are told to be, they put you in the "hole" and then take you out only one hour each day, to let you see the daylight through a prison cage.

Prisoners are counted at 3 am, 5 am, 9 am, 4 pm, 9 pm and midnight, because they are afraid that we might escape. It's funny how, when we are outside in the yard and some fog sets in, they immediately send us to our prison cells and count us again.

Many people work in prison, but 60 percent of the jobs are unnecessary. Prison is the last stepping-stone of a human. If you survive prison, you can live anywhere. It is worse to be a prisoner than to be dead, because the dead don't see or hear, don't suffer or feel pain. It's tragic to be trapped with 1,500 men, or to take a shower in your shoes with 10 men.

Time doesn't go by in prison. In prison you shouldn't talk with other people because there are many traitors. The less they know about you the better off you are. Prisoners should be united, but they are not. You should never forget and leave your closet open because if somebody doesn't like you and puts something in it that you shouldn't have, they'll put you in "the hole." Also they can increase your sentence by up to 10 percent as punishment.

Many people try to hear or learn something about

you, in order to betray you so they may reduce their own sentence.

The staff in prison could behave in a better way, but it's the first time in their life they've got some power and they abuse it. The prisoners have no rights. If a guard criticizes you, even when they are wrong, you have no right to disagree. All you can do is obey and apologize in the end. The food we eat here is what the rest of society throws away. We are told that prisons spend large amounts of money for the prisoners. It might be true because all the food goes into the garbage since they don't want to cook it properly so we might be able to actually eat it.

I have now been in prison for 10 months and so far not even one politician has come here to ask us about the circumstances we live in and why we are here. If somebody ever does come, they stay at the outer gate and then leave.

One day, while we were having lunch, they gave us

Coca-Cola. I asked them what this special treat is today and they said that some government official had come to visit the prison. I guess they spend the money on our food, trying to give us healthy stuff so they prefer to give us water instead of Coke, to protect our health. What do you think? Don't they do that to protect our health?

The building where we live is a two story one. The dimensions are 160 feet long and 60 feet wide. It has 64 prison cells, with dimensions 8 by 11 feet each and 3 people live in each one without any doors. There's no private time. The security guard is allowed to check us any time he/she wants. Whenever he is bored of sitting, he comes over, demands you to get out of your prison cell and starts searching everything. If he finds something that is not sold in the prison's shop (Commissary), it is picked up and thrown away. If they find something "serious," you are put in "the hole."

The circumstances in prison could be much

better, but instead they become worse every day. In my opinion, the only good thing is that the prison is hot during winter and cold during summer. At least we don't freeze to death in the winter or get heat exhaustion in the summer.

I think it would be best if nobody knows exactly what day you'll leave prison. Even your best friends should only find out on the morning of your release because people here in prison are jealous of your impending freedom and they might try and harm you. They have nothing to lose because they have to stay in prison for many years. Also, they will try to get you in some kind of trouble so you don't leave when you are supposed to.

Another thing, if you are in trouble with the authorities, you'd better tell them everything you know right from the beginning. Because in the end they will get everything they want from you.

When you fill out your papers for court, if you tell them that you are addicted to drugs they'll put you in a rehab program and you will save 15 months from your sentence.

Nobody will tell you a word about this drug rehab program. Nobody told me about it. I heard about rehab one week before I went to prison and this small piece of advice cost me $6,000.

When they place you under arrest, it's better for you not to say anything at all without a lawyer present. Because they will distort everything you say and will cause you more trouble. So stay silent.

The currency in prison is in the manner of postage stamps. I pay 6 stamps to have my clothes washed and 2 stamps for each piece I want ironed. I can do all this by myself, but I wanted to help some of the prisoners in here. They need the stamps more than I do. For anything we need here, instead of money we exchange it for stamps. If you have money in your account here, you can buy from the "Commissary". We can go there once a week. You are only allowed $300 in your account per month for purchases. We are given 300 telephone minutes each month. Each minute costs 23 cents.

We are allowed to have visits in prison 5 times a week: Monday, Saturday and Sunday from 8.30 am until 3.00 pm. Thursday and Friday from 2.30 pm until 8 pm. You are eligible to have visits 12 times a month. The visits on Saturdays and Sundays count double. The visitors can be up to 6 people each time.

There is something else you should know that is very important. Many people travel a very long distance to visit their relatives or friends in prison and they are not allowed to get in. The reason is that sometimes they check people's hands with a device that scans for drugs. Once in a while the device can sound the alarm without you ever having touched any drugs. It sounds the alarm because you might have touched money that had some drug powder on it, or maybe nothing at all. It's a machine, so it is bound to make mistakes.

That's why you should wash your hands well

before coming to visitation. If the anti-drug device sounds the alarm, they kick you out and you are not allowed to visit for the next 48 hours for the first offense, for a whole month the second time, for three months the third time, and six months the fourth time. If you test positive a fifth time you can never come back to visit.

The thing that brings the most joy to a prisoner is when someone comes to visit them.

Prisoners who are accused of a felony lose many of their rights. When I accepted the deal, I had no idea that they would take these rights for the rest of my life. My lawyers said nothing about this. I had no idea what a felony was.

I didn't know that the government would see me as its enemy for the rest of my life.. If somebody from my family goes to prison, I won't be allowed to visit them. If one of my loved ones is convicted of a felony, I'm not allowed to talk to them. It is almost impossible to get life insurance with a felony on your record. And if I ever get life insurance, I'll have to pay double or triple what anyone else would. I'm not allowed to own a gun to protect my family home.

If this situation continues everybody will be charged with a felony. Before we tell somebody "Good Morning" we'll have to ask them for evidence that they haven't committed a felony. That's why the government should say "enough with this cruel punishment" and give these people back their rights so that they can rebuild their lives. Instead of dividing these people, they should help them rejoin society. After all, these people have paid their debt to society.

The things that I have seen here will only be forgotten when my heart stops beating. After one year in prison, everything has started to look the same. It is a monotonous and mind numbing environment.

Today, April 3 of 2005, I was finally told when exactly I'll get out of prison. I was told that I'm getting out on April 17th instead of March 21st with no explanation as to why. If we count those extra 1-2 months for each one of the 3 million people who are in prison the total time served will be more than 300 years. But nothing in society will change because of this. The results will be the same. Everything happens for profit. That's why the prisons have to be full.

In prison you have to be careful about everything you say or do, to avoid problems. Good character matters the most, because it shows who you really are. And good character is what gets you through any potential problem in here.

It's not like your reputation, which is something other people assign to you. Many people here ask me, "Why don't they wake you up at 4 am to test your urine to see if there are any drugs in your system, and why haven't they ever put you in the hole?"

I reply to them, "I'll never go to the hole, because they respect me." Then they say that I'm lucky.

I've met a lot of people in prison who have told me the stories of their suffering and how unjustly the government has treated them. Their pain is huge and their agony for their children and their loved ones is intense.

Some prisoners fill out forms 6 months in advance so they can send a small gift to their kids for Christmas.

Yesterday, somebody came to my cell and asked me if I had any chore for him to do so he might earn a few stamps to send his wife so she could send him a letter.

"Do you mean that your wife doesn't have any stamps to send you a letter?" I asked him.

He said that she didn't have any, because when he went to prison, 8 months ago, she was pregnant and just now gave birth. She cannot work because she has three more kids and lives with her mother.

I asked him why he was in prison and he told me

something unbelievable.

He was a hunter and went hunting, but it was illegal to kill deer at the time. It was not the season for hunting deer. The FBI had put a fake deer in the forest and he shot it. Then they arrested him and put him in jail.

An inmate here was previously in prison for 15 years. When he got out he tried to find a job but no one would hire him. He couldn't even rent an apartment because of his prior record. One day he ended up back in prison. When I asked him why he was brought back to prison, he said that he had stolen a bike for his daughter.

Another one stole a $2 box of batteries but because of the fact he had the label of "felon," he was sentenced to life in prison. I saw this on CNN.

Somebody else told me that he was accused of selling drugs. He was never caught with any drugs and he never accepted any deal. So he went to court to get vindicated from these false charges. He saw two "witnesses" there, whom he had never seen before. They claimed that he had sold them drugs. Finally, the "jury of his peers" decided that he and his wife were guilty. Then they were taken away and everything they owned was confiscated. The man was sentenced to 30 years and his wife to 27. They left behind four kids to be put out on the streets.

Another inmate told me that he was sentenced to life; his mother was sentenced to 30 years, his sister 28 years, and his grandmother to 27 years. They were all convicted of "conspiracy".

A young guy came to my cell one day and told me that he saw in a magazine a commercial about a liquid that can be dropped in a drink to make you sexually aroused. He ordered it and when he went to the post of-fice to pick it up, he was arrested and sent to prison for 5 years. According to him, the FBI had posted the adver-tisement as a trap.

Yet another man was put in prison for 3 years be-cause he went to the FBI himself in order to protect his friend's wife. This is his story.

One day his friend told him, "I want you to kill my wife because she took everything from me when we divorced."

So he said, "Are you crazy? What are you talking about?"

And then his friend said, "If you don't do it, I've got somebody else who will."

So, this guy, in order to protect the woman, said "OK," and took the gun and put it in his car. Afterwards he took the gun to the FBI and a week later they called him to go to their office. When he got there, he was told that he should record his friend saying that he wanted him to kill his wife. The man told the FBI agents that this wasn't his job, it was theirs. They replied that he didn't understand the situation. They said that now this was his job also and if he didn't record this conversation he'd be arrested. Then he told them to do whatever they liked and left. Two weeks later, while he was at the doctor for some exams, they came in and arrested him. He had served in the Army, so he thought that he'd find justice. After the lawyers took $100,000 from him they finally told him that he should cut a deal and go to prison for "only" 3 years. The lawyers said if he went to court he'd lose and would get 10 years. He nearly went insane but there was no other solution. He accepted the deal and he's now in prison.

My friends, there are many traps everywhere.

Whatever looks great is not necessarily great. You need to be careful.

Young men and women, I'm telling you to be very careful about the people you date, who they are and where they work. Danger is everywhere and you might end up in prison just by being associated with the wrong person.

Shame on the Culprits

In 1998, a first cousin of mine, who was my most beloved one, called me from Greece. His father had brought us to America, and he and his brother helped us because we had nobody else those days. That's why he became my most beloved relative.

He asked me to help him come to America with his family, in order to work here with his son and wife and make some money.

He said to me he wanted to retire after he came here. He was 58 years old and as always, I agreed to help him.

When they came to the United States, I went to the bank and took out a loan of $15,000, to help him get started. With this money he rented an apartment and bought a car. He had spent his entire life running a kafenió (coffee shop), so he bought another one and opened for business. When he bought it, we all started going there to support him. After ten months, l went to my restaurant as usual and found him there with his wife and son.

As I sat down and greeted him, he said, "We are leaving for Greece; here are the keys to the kafenió."

I felt like I just got struck by lightning and I asked him if he was kidding me, but he had already made his decision.

"We have already left the apartment and we have all our personal items with us in the hotel," he said. "Tomorrow morning we are leaving for Greece."

"Didn't you say that you'll stay here until you retire?" I said. "Why don't you stay here a little bit longer to make some more money"?

Then he told me that he had made more money than I could ever imagine. And when I asked him if he had paid off the bank's loan, he told me "You'll have to pay off the loan."

So he left for Greece and I was stuck with the kafenió. I tried to find somebody to sell it to so I could pay off the loan.

After a week, a man who owned the kafenió equipment came over and asked me where my cousin was. I told him that my cousin left for Greece permanently. Then he said that my cousin owed him $30,000. I suggested that he take ownership of the kafenió and possibly make some of his money back. He agreed to take it, so I gave him the keys. Three days later he picked up his equipment from the kafenió and left. I had to find another buyer. So two weeks later, I sold it to somebody for $10,000. I paid $5,000 more and settled with the bank. After six months had passed the man who owned the kafenió came to my restaurant and told my son,

"I'm not busy at the kafenió."

"Do you want to go and work there after 5 pm and whatever you bring in, we can split it?"

My son agreed and started working there.

In the past, my cousins and I used to play music

and sing in our homes.

Right then we were given the opportunity to enjoy our hobby, so every Saturday we started going to the kafenió to play music. One night a friend of mine said, "We might put a table up there in that corner and play poker." I didn't want to be rude to him, so I said 'ok'. Then one game became another and we finally ended up having three games per week. Before that nobody would step foot in the kafenió but now it was full of people. I'm telling you the truth, I really wanted to leave the kafenió but I didn't know how.

Some "friends" were jealous of us and wanted to close the kafenió. The second week we were there, somebody brought two undercover cops to the kafenió. They played on the poker machines and a young guy paid them the money they won. They should have taken the machines and closed the kafenió because according to the law, the guy shouldn't have paid them any money. But they didn't do so. They had bigger plans for us.

Those jealous Greeks would call the police every now and then and tell them many lies about the kafenió. They claimed that in the kafenió there were drugs, that we sold alcohol without having a liquor license, that we had three cops for protection and many other false things. When the police called the FBI and told them about the kafenió, the FBI replied that this was local police business and not theirs. But those Greeks didn't stop calling the police. In the meantime, my son had cop friends he grew up with and they would visit the kafenió sometimes. Maybe that's why they said there were three policemen protecting it. So the police called the FBI again and told them that we had an illegal establishment under police protection.

This bogus investigation lasted for 18 months, so they had the time to turn the wrong into right and the false into truth. They finally incriminated 22 innocent people and sent them to prison. They told incredible lies, to the point of saying that we used to beat people in order to collect money they owed us.

I never hung out with anyone in the whole case. They had no evidence against me but they charged me with the biggest accusation of all: that I was the leader of all those people, that I was the one who gave the orders to those people who did all the illegal activities and that the kafenió was the place where we made all the decisions. They also tried to get my son to sell drugs, but he didn't agree. If he had agreed to do so, he would never be free again.

A poll was conducted in a prison in Florida on "the war on drugs," showed that 99 out of 100 women had been looking at a sentence of 20 years to life for being arrested for the first time. Twenty years in prison for only selling drugs without any guns being involved.

I want to say that drugs are very dangerous not only because they destroy our health, but also because they are illegal. According to the law, the risk for someone to get in trouble is always present even if they are not involved in drugs. When you are around drugs, it's easy for you to get in trouble. If I went to prison then everyone has the possibility of going to prison.

That's how this icy and dark morning came, on December 5th of 2002, when they invaded our house like another Hitler and took us from our beds and lead us to jail with no reason. That day they destroyed 22 families. Those two Greeks from the FBI may be proud of what they've done, but they should keep in mind that there's a God who may punish them some day for their actions.

The Battles Against HIV-AIDS

My friends, two days ago, on October 14th of 2005, I had to go to the doctor to give a blood sample and be tested for AIDS. This happens in all prisons. Before I got out of there, I asked the doctor if I should go there again when they have the results. He said: "You don't have to come again if you are not positive for AIDS. In case you have AIDS, they'll call you from the loud speakers."

After a week, at 7 am, they called my name to go to the doctor's office. I'm telling the truth, I felt like someone had cut me off at the knees. Crazy thoughts were running through my mind.

I was telling myself, "I went through so many troubles and I've been waiting for so long and with so much agony for that day when I'll go back home to find my life again. What if they tell me that I have AIDS?"

That would definitely destroy me.

When I got there, the doctor told me that I was healthy and he gave me a paper to sign. I was so happy that I totally forgot I was in prison for a moment.

After experiencing this fearful ordeal, I thought I should research this fatal disease more. By researching and studying I learned a lot of things.

The sanctity of sex between us and the respect for our family doesn't allow us to talk about stuff like that. People don't know how serious AIDS is and how we contract it.

Our planet suffers nowadays from this disease and there is no cure yet. Our only way to prevent ourselves of getting this virus is to avoid dangerous relationships and use protection. This virus kills all the white cells in our system that tries to fight it. The white cells cannot kill this virus, so finally the virus kills them all.

AIDS is being spread through three means; through sex, through blood and through a pregnant woman to her baby. The easiest way though for someone to get it is through sex.

Science is not sure if AIDS can be spread through kisses, but we should be careful about kisses, just in case there is an injury in the mouth cavity.

Another source is hypodermic needles and blood transfusions. Most pregnant women who have the virus will give it to their babies. There is only a small percentage of 2% that will not give it to their babies if they use the medicine, AZT, and if they give birth through Caesarean section. Unfortunately it's also being transferred through the mother's breast milk.

AIDS is not transmitted through hugs, sweat, tears, sneezing, coughing, or toilet use. Also, we are not in danger if we live in the same place with someone who has the virus.

You are not safe though, if you use the same toothbrush or the same razor as someone who is infected.

All the people who have the HIV virus won't necessarily get sick from AIDS, but all the people who have

AIDS have the HIV virus.

The HIV virus is the beginning of the end for our body and the AIDS is the end.

It usually takes HIV 10 years to turn into AIDS, but nowadays we have better medicine and that's why it can take up to 15 years for somebody to get sick.

There are many people who have the HIV virus and live a normal life. Fifty-percent of people with HIV who take their medication, don't smoke, and exercise a lot stay alive for many years just carrying the HIV virus.

In 2000, one million Americans had HIV and in 2005 the number increased up to 2.2 million.

Every year in America 40,000 people get the virus.

AIDS is the most fatal virus for men and women between the ages of 25 to 44.

Up until April of 2000, 438,795 Americans died from AIDS, of whom 374,422 were men and 64,373 were women.

Up Until the end of 2000, 36.1 million people in

the whole world got the virus. Most of them live in the Third World. By the end of 2000, 21.8 million people died from AIDS in the whole world.

In America now 1 out of 150 people lives with HIV. First is New York City, California comes next, and North Carolina, where I live, is tenth.

My dear friends, it's not worth it for someone to suffer like that. That's why you should protect yourself properly and keep away from this fatal disease so that we all can live a full life.

About the Earthquakes and the Tsunamis

Today, December 26 of 2004, the big earthquake and tsunami happened in the Indian Ocean. Who could ever imagine that the sea would come on land and kill hundreds of thousands of people! It's a big tragedy and who knows what our eyes will see next. Today we are taught what we are supposed to do in case of a big earthquake. "We have to forget the things we used to know and used to learn," says a famous American rescuer.

The things that we used to learn in the past were that, in case of an earthquake, if you are at school, you'll have to hide under desks or tables. If you are at home, you'd better hide under beds and if you are outside, hide under cars.

All those theories are now nullified because of the American rescuer who says: "all those people who hid themselves under tables and beds are all dead." In a building in Mexico which collapsed during the big earthquake of 1985, there was a school. All of the kids died but they could have survived if they had lain down next to the desks and along the corridors.

The rescuer says: "When a building falls on objects, they leave some empty space next to them."

In the earthquake of San Francisco of 1989, all the people who stayed in their cars were killed but they would have survived if they had gotten out of their cars and lain next to them.

Many times here in prison the guards put two tables outside the cafeteria and collect charitable contributions for tsunami and Katrina victims. All the prisoners line up to give whatever they can afford from the little money their families send them. Each one gives from $5 up to $20. That money is a big deal for prisoners because they need it for themselves.

The unjust thing is that I never heard anyone say one word about it. If each prisoner gives 10 dollars, 30 million dollars will be gathered. There are 3 million people in prison nowadays.

I've heard on the radio about donations from other sources, but nobody ever says a word about this huge offering from the prisoners. And that's not enough. If somebody says something about a prisoner, it is always something negative.

I want those who hide the truth to know that the people of this country do know the truth. Almost everybody has a loved one in prison. Seventy percent of the population is in a virtual prison because they are the victims of the crooks who work in the government.

Like I said before, nobody wants the real criminals to be free. Neither do I. But the real criminals are not in prisons yet they commit horrendous crimes.

I wonder how many millions of people this system needs to destroy before it stops.

If people could only speak openly we would never be in this situation. People are afraid though, because, if they tell the truth, they will be thrown in prison again.

171

I hope someday this catastrophe stops and we live again in the compassionate and true America that we knew before.

Today America is like a rotten red apple, beautiful outside with worms inside.

It's sad, but it's the truth.

The Dead Cannot Save Us

Friends and relatives of mine sent me a lot of religious books while I'm in prison. They send me icons of saints whom I've never seen and they assure me that they pray for me in their churches. Most of the people here in prison ask me if I believe in Jesus and they hold a *Bible* in their hands. About 80% of them are in prison for drugs.

I wonder why and how people in our country got to this point. Half of them are lined up in a corner, looking for drugs that will lift them up and the other half of them are lined up in a church praying to find their place in Heaven. Actually they all seek the same thing, somebody to save them. All those people are fanatics and need help.

I don't understand how we have no idea where we came from, but we know where we are going. Don't you think that we should first get to know ourselves? We don't know where we are, so why are we looking for another place to go? When we don't know where we are and we are willing to go somewhere else, how can we go there? Maybe we are already there and we don't know it.

The purpose and the mission of Jesus Christ was to make us believe in ourselves and to teach us the commandments of God.

He first taught us of the many good traits we have as humans. The things that those religious people tell us though seem to have traumatized our brains and we cannot think clearly.

We easily say "we are nothing" and we look for supernatural help desperately. Who is the man who taught us that we are nothing?

We are nothing when we allow somebody else to tell us that we are nothing. If we are really nothing, why don't we jump off a cliff and put an end to all this? But we refuse to do so, because deep down we know that this is not true and we don't believe in all those lies.

They teach us to depend only on God and not on ourselves. Please, don't disregard your desires and God's will by acting like that. The outcome of our lives depends on our decisions. They tell us that we cannot understand what the *Bible* says, that we should pray to all the icons that humans make and not to speak at all because we-are not pure enough.

My friends, why are we asking saints to save us? Why are we praising names of saints when we are living in the real life? The dead saints cannot help us, neither can they save us.

The people who asked the saints to help them in the past did that because in those days those holy men were alive. It wasn't the holy men who saved people though, it was the smart and nice words that they said to people giving them faith and strength to save themselves on their own. Men with such strong personalities live and die, come and go. But the wisdom of life lived, lives and will live forever.

Try to find living people who think like them. Living people can give you an answer, but the dead cannot speak. Walk along with those people who are living.

We consider the people who lived in the past as heroes and we mention their names often, but we make fun of those who are pure and are living. We degrade them. We kill them or we throw them in prisons. When they die, we will be the ones who will praise them.

Why all this hypocrisy? When people die, they are considered saints, but while they are still alive, they are our enemies. When they die we glorify them, but while they are living, we curse them.

We ask the dead to save us because they cannot talk to us, but if we ask the people who are alive to save us they'll talk to us about our mistakes. That's why we don't talk to them.

We are hypocrites and we need to find ourselves. A true friend has to tell you the truth about yourself. Now I will answer to them who ask me if I believe in Jesus. Of course I believe in all of them, because I believe in God who sent them, but I believe that all those were smart on their own.

I believe that all people have the strength and the intelligence to understand where we are nowadays. I believe that God will accept you if you are pure and will forgive your mistakes. If you choose to live with Satan though, and you are not honest with God, then He will punish you in due time.

So let's allow the dead to talk with the dead and the living to talk with the living.

People talk about miracles here and there. They say that a holy icon burst into tears. Some people say that this is a lie and some others believe it's true.

My dear friends, if we take a look around us, we'll see many miracles. No one speaks of them though. We see a flower bloom and we admire its beauty or its scent, yet it came out of mud. The water cycle: Water falls to the earth as rain. Then it drains into the rivers, streams, lakes, and ultimately into the oceans. Then it evaporates and goes back to the sky as clouds. The water cycle purifies water for us over and over again into infinity.

These are miracles for me.

My Life with the Artists

I was 12 years old, in Greece, when a cousin of mine came from the Queen's technical schools. He brought with him a record player with batteries because in those days the village didn't have electricity. He also brought with him two small records and I heard the song "These dirty hands" of singer Stelios Kazantzidis and the song "Like the cursed one" of singer Stratos Kyprios for the first time. It was the first time I heard "bouzouki" songs and I loved them. They were singing like songbirds.

I stayed at my cousin's house all night listening to those songs. Those days we only listened to songs in the festivals. We didn't even have a radio. I was so amazed by the deep words, the beautiful voices and the wonderful music. After two weeks, my cousin left and took those discs with him.

In 1967, when I was in America, a Greek man came to my work and was selling records with Greek music. I didn't have any money, so I was looking at them from a distance. He understood that and said, "If you want, take whatever you like and you can pay me when you have money."

Then I went there to take a look and I was very moved by the titles. I bought four records: "In a foreign land since childhood," and "How much I miss my village" by singer Stelios Kazantzidis, "I tear my passport" by Manolis Angelopoulos, "I was born a villager" by Stratos Kyprios. I bought a record player and every night I stayed up listening to those songs and crying.

Figure 26 - The Author with a favorite singer in Greece, Manoli Agelopoulo - 1983

I found where the record seller's house was and I became his best customer. When I got back to Greece, I went to Monastiraki place directly. I spent all my money on records. I remember people were asking me, "Do you want to hear this song?" Then I asked them, "Who is the singer?" When they said that it was Kazantzidis or Aggelopoulos, I told them, "I only want to know the title. I don't need to listen to the song."

If I didn't have the specific record, I bought it, because I knew that all the songs were really wonderful.

Since then, I filled up my record collection with the best "bouzouki" singers and with the best known Greek songs. I like the folk songs as well. What can I say about the unforgettable Takis Karnavas, the king of folk songs, the hero of Xeromero. He definitely deserves praise.

When I was placed on "probation" after getting out of prison and my eyes were full of tears, I got in my car and heard a song by Karnavas:

"If you see rivers with waters, that water the fields,
It's my eyes that are full of tears and cry.
If you see mountains burning the crests of hills breaking
It's because of the pain in my heart, in my broken heart.
Oh heart, stay strong, because we need to get through this
pain,
To find a cold fountain and cool our soul in its water"

When the singer Karnavas died, I heard the bad news from my friend Kostas Aristopoulos, because the media said nothing about it.

In my record collection I have about 5,000 songs. In my life, wherever I go, I ask people if they have records and if they have something I don't have, I buy it at whatever the cost.

In 1980, in Kalyvia village, close to Agrinio, I bought the song "With sweat and blood" by the singer Kazantzidis for 20,000 drachmas.

In 1984, I went to the radio station of Mesologgi and I asked them to let me see all the songs that people requested on the radio. I found some songs I didn't have in my collection, but they could not send them to me. Then I asked them to play them for me the next day so that I might record them and that's what they did.

In 1986, in Agrinio, I visited some stores and there was an old lady there. I asked her if she had any records. She said, "My child, there are some records over there. Take a look if you like."

I found the songs "Tonight I'll sing painfully with

a sweet voice" and "Man, why?" I had to have them and I offered her $50 for each song.

Then she said, "In that case, I'll give them to you and my husband can buy new discs."

These songs are my life and maybe some people may make fun of me. They say "give Dimitrios songs and take from him whatever you want...."

That's the truth. I believe that singing has to do with our character. If you want to become a good singer, then the songs you sing should represent you. You should sing the songs for yourself first and then sing them as a singer.

The best songs are those which represent simple people, the people who struggle for their living, those who are in pain, who have lost a love, and who are in love.

I was always willing to personally meet all those famous artists and to listen to them sing, but it was difficult because I lived in America and whenever I went to

Greece they were not performing anywhere.

This had always frustrated me and my friends kept telling me not to try in vain because those singers would never accept me if I went to visit them. First on my list was Stelios Kazantzidis and he was the most difficult to visit because he didn't sing in taverns anymore.

Other people told me that if those singers could not gain something from you, then they would hardly talk to you. I replied to them: "They won't talk with me about money because I don't have any!"

The same happens with politicians. If you want to see a politician, people say that they won't accept you. In 1986, I was in Athens and one morning I got prepared to go to Kastri to see the Prime Minister, Andreas Papandreou. My sister convinced me not to go because she said he wouldn't meet me.

I didn't think this was true. I am sure that if I had gone there I would have met him. In this life if you don't try to accomplish something, you lose 100 percent of the time. I believe that in order to rule people, you should first love them. In order to sing for people, you should first love them. Only in this way will people think highly of you and praise you throughout history. The artists and politicians have to come from the simple people and represent the simple people. How can they kick you out when you go visit them? Their fans are their life.

Singing is a blessing to our society and we are lucky to belong to this generation where some of the best Greek songs came from. Today young people, although they are special, don't participate in singing as much as the older people did in the past. Personally, if I listen to a song and don't understand the lyrics, I turn off the radio.

In 2002, I was in Athens and my nieces wanted to go to listen to Giannis Ploutarchos, but it was very difficult to reserve a table for Saturday night. So I asked Dimitris Xanthakis if his son, who sang there, could book seats for us. When we arrived there, everything was pleasant and then the singer Ploutarchos showed up.

He made a great appearance on stage. He was a good singer and, according to what my friends say, he is also a nice guy. Two hours passed by and I couldn't understand one word, so to make sure I wasn't going deaf, I asked Xanthakis,

"Dimitri, can you understand what the singer is singing about?"

"Not even a word," he said.

I have a problem with the songs of our times. Maybe I am spoiled by the old singers. I would buy a cassette and all the songs were perfect. The folkloric bouzouki singing has to survive because it gives people strength and comforts their pain. I believe that the music should not be louder than the singer's voice. Otherwise the people cannot appreciate the lyrics.

In 1987, coming back from Greece, I brought with me 26 boxes of records and cassettes. The customs agents were concerned because they could not believe all those were mine. They thought that I wanted to sell them for profit.

In 1979, I had a tavern in Agrinio and one day, while I was making a "kokoretsi," a friend of mine brought me a magazine, the "Treasure."

On the front page I saw the picture of Stelios Kazantzidis and it said that he had opened a factory to produce Ouzo, with the title "Yparcho" (I exist). Immediately I thought that I should go to Thessalonica to meet him. I posted a paper on my tavern's door: "Closed, because I've gone to Thessalonica to meet Stelios Kazantzidis."

I took my father and a friend of mine and we traveled together. We passed Ioannina, Metsovo, Larissa and we arrived at Thessalonica. I found his factory and asked a guy to tell me the truth. I said that I was coming from far away only to meet Stelios. I asked him if Stelios was there and he said, "He comes here many times, but now he's not here. He might come tomorrow morning." The next day I went to the factory again, but Stelios wasn't there. Then I asked the same guy where I might find Stelios and he said, "He might be at Agios Konstantinos beach close, to Kammena Vourla."

I thanked him for the information and I left for Agios Konstantinos. I got there at 3 pm and I took a route that led me to the sea. I told my father and my friend, "You guys stay here and I'll walk all the way to the sea to find Stelios. If I find him, I will come back to show you the way."

I walked 2 or 3 kilometers and then I saw a hut. Outside of the hut I saw a man sitting alone. My heart started beating fast because I thought he might be Stelios Kazantzidis. I said to myself "now is the time I've been waiting for since I was a child." I took a deep breath and went ahead. I opened the gate of the fence and went in. When he saw me he stood up from his chair and as I approached him, I asked: "Are you Stelios Kazantzidis?"

"Who are you?" He said with a smile.

Then I hugged him and said, "You don't know me, but I know you very well."

189

"Where are you coming from and for what reason?" He asked me again and I answered him,

"I am an immigrant who stayed up many nights listening to your songs and my dream was to meet you in person some day."

I told him that I passed by Thessalonica and I had brought him a taste of a new Ouzo made by a new factory. He laughed and said, "Come, come on in and sit down."

Then I brought my father and my friend and Stelios introduced us to his mother and to Miss Vasso. He wasn't married to Miss Vasso, yet. After a while the table was covered by cooked fish caught by Stelios himself.

After we finished our dinner, my father said to Stelios, "What did you do to my son that he was looking all over Greece to find you?"

Stelios turned to me with a smile and said, "Dimitri, why are you that determined to find me?"

"I want to ask you a huge favor," I said. "Every

190

time I come to Greece, I want to come visit you and I want us to become friends forever."

He looked at me carefully and said, "What I'm going to tell you, without even knowing where you come from, I say to very few people. The door of my house will be always open for you."

Figure 27 - The Author's biggest day back in 1979 when he meets his favorite singer in Greece, Stelio Kazantzioi

He kept his word until the end of his life. I remember one day I was working at the restaurant and the telephone rang. When I picked up the phone, it was Stelios.

"How are you doing, Dimitris?"

I asked him who he was, as I always do on the phone. "It's me, Stelios, don't you recognize me?"

"I recognized you," I said, "but I couldn't believe that Kazantzidis himself is calling me."

"Why are you saying this? Aren't we friends?" he said.

Many friends of mine begged me to have them meet Stelios. I sent some of them to see him and whenever they went to his home, he always accepted them and offered them dinner. When they asked him why he treated them so nicely, he told them: "Once you are Dimitris' friends, you are friends of mine as well."

Of course nothing happened without Miss Vasso's help. Whenever I went to Miss Vasso's home, she always prepared dinner for us.

In 1995, I was in Lamia and I visited Stelios. We sat around the table in his yard. He brought a barrel of olives, a barrel of pepper pickles, one with feta cheese, a bottle of 'tsipouro' and he started telling jokes,

"Once upon a time, Karagiozis (the main figure of the Greek 'shadow theater') and Hantzatzaris decided to open a store, but they had no money. So they went to Barba-Giorgo and asked for 100 drachmas. He said to them: 'Ok my children, but I want my money back tonight.' They took the money and bought a barrel of Ouzo that cost 99 drachmas. They went to a crossroad, put the ouzo in a corner of the street and started walking up and down waiting for customers. The time passed by and after no customers, Karagiozis went to Hatzantzaris with the 1 drachma that was left. 'I have only 1 drachma. Can you please give me a glass of ouzo?'

'Of course,' Hatzantzaris said, 'whatever my customer wants will be done' and gave him the ouzo drink. He took the drachma. After a while Hatzantzaris went to Karagiozis and said, 'Karagiozis, I have a drachma, will you give me a glass of ouzo?' So they gave the drachma to each other several times until they drank the whole ouzo, got drunk, put on some music and danced the *vanti maestro*. The same night Barba-Giorgo came to them to get his 100 drachmas back but they didn't have it. He beat them senseless and closed the store."

Figure 28 - The Author with Stelio Kazantzio and his cousin, Vasili

I had one main problem with Stelios: he never allowed me to pay. In 2000, when I visited him, I found him with my friend Kostas Katambas. After we met, he gave us a ride to the famous tavern of Koumbouras to have some dinner. I always had other people with me, because everyone wanted to see Stelios. In the tavern we were given all types of food. I remember once I went in the kitchen to give the girls who cooked the food 100 drachmas and they told me if they accepted the money, Stelios would be very mad at them. I could never convince them to take the money.

I had many unforgettable moments with Stelios.

When I was with him, I was the happiest man on earth and I forgot all my worries. Every single time that Stelios made a new music disc he sent it to me and wrote wishes on it for me and my family. I constantly asked him to go on tour so that people can enjoy him. He replied: "When I make the decision, we'll go together."

I remember one day he said to me, "If I am singing on stage, I'll have to sing from beginning to end, because people never let me take a break and I can't let them down either."

Stelios was a unique person. He lived in his own world. He became an orphan at a very young age and lived in poverty and under rough conditions. He tried to make a living on the streets.

On Athenas street he sold water to the laborers for tips. He had a flask with water wrapped in a wet cloth to keep it cold. Many times he didn't have enough money to take the bus home. In winter, he kept warm by sleeping on the stairs of Omonoia square next to the truck engines. That's why when he sang, his eyes would water with every song he sang.

He loved children very much and always lowered his head to talk to them. Once I was at his home in the suburb of Athens, Pefki, when the bell rang. Five children had seen Stelios' name on the bell and rang it. He went, opened the door and talked to them. One of the kids gave him a card from his father's tavern inviting him for dinner.

He loved his brother, Stathis, and his family. Stelios scolded Stathis for smoking and would send him to the balcony to smoke. Both brothers loved each other very much.

In September of 2000 I was with my son Kostas in Greece and we visited Stelios. Stelios prepared a dinner for us and my son saw Stelios for the first time. While we were eating he turned to me and said: "Father, I came to Greece. Now that I have met Stelios, this is Greece for me."

Stelios was shocked to hear him say that. My son turned to Stelios and said, "If I have children some day, now I know how to raise them well."

Stelios asked him 'how' and my son said: "I'll just have them listen to your songs."

Stelios was the singer whom all Greeks loved. He was loved by people of all ages, young and old. He sang about the pain, the bitterness, and the joy of people.

He loved people as well. Whether he spoke or

sang, his voice was pure. That's why Greeks all over the world adored him. Of course maybe Mr. Notis Sfakiana-kis, whom I love and respect, doesn't agree with all this. Every time he speaks in public though, he messes up. He says: "Greeks are losers. Greeks in the USA are dis-hwashers. For me Kazantzidis is not what he is for other Greeks. He was just another talented singer. Stelios was not real because he spoke differently and Andreas Papan-dreou, the previous Greek Prime Minister, destroyed Greece."

I will say only a few things for those who are not alive anymore and can't defend themselves.

Unforgettable Andreas Papandreou was one of the cleverest politicians in our country and had many skills. When he spoke, his words were powerful. He did many things for Greeks and Greece. It's such a pity that he left us and now Greeks are poorer without Andreas Papan-dreou and Stelios Kazantzidis.

When Stelios got sick, I called Ms Ioanna, Stathis'

wife, to find out the truth. And she said: "Dimitri, I can't lie to you. We are losing Stelios, because this fatal disease has spread throughout his body, including his head.

We didn't talk very long because she was very depressed. Every time I called him, he asked me, "Will you come and see me?"

He would always break my heart by telling me this. I finally went to Greece, only for a week, to see Stelios for the last time. When I got to the airport of Athens, Stathis was waiting for me and we left for Stelios' home. When we got there, Stelios hugged me and sat next to me. We talked for a bit, but he was in pain. I told him that my trip was dedicated to him. I would go only for one day to my village to visit my parents and I'd come back to Athens. He said 'ok' and I left the next day. This would be the last time I spoke to Stelios.

When I got back from my village, Mrs. Vasso told me that after I left for the village, Stelios never got up from his bed again. After that I went to his room and sat next to him for a long time. He didn't even open his eyes one time. I was very sad and asked Mrs. Vasso to call me if Stelios opened his eyes. I went to his home five days in a row, but he never opened his eyes. I put my hands on his shoulders, but this huge star never opened his eyes. It seems like he was tired of fighting for his life and let go. Then in my mind came the lyrics from one of his songs: *"Even if you cry for me now, even if you feel pity for me, it's too late; you'll never see me again in this world,"*

Then I kissed him 'good bye' on his forehead and left. When I got to my hotel, I went to a store to buy a newspaper. When I went to pay for it, the man told me, "Take whatever you like and leave. When I saw Stelios on your jacket, my heart broke. This man is my life,"

I had a picture of Stelios in a heart pin on my jacket. "I just came from his house" I said.

He came close to me and asked me, "Tell me, how is he?"

"Our beloved star is not gonna sing again." I took

off the heart pin with Stelios' picture and gave it to him.

When I got back to America, I called Mrs. Vasso in the hospital and she gave me Stelios, to hear his voice for the last time. I said to him, "Stelios, don't give up. A miracle might happen."

After two weeks, at 11 am, my friend Dimitris Hionas called me: "We lost Stelios Kazantzidis, our brother."

Dimitris knew how much I worried. That's why he called me first.

In 2002, I went to Greece and my first stop was at Stelios' unforgettable house in Elefsina and after that I left for my village.

I was there when my friend, Kostas Katambas, called me: "Stelios' last will was to make 20 gold medals with his picture on them and give them to his friends whom he chose. One of those is yours."

I thanked him and he finally gave me a gold medal and a silver one. Those are precious pieces for me Stelios will live forever. People die and are forgotten by the living.

Stelios will never be forgotten and will always live in our hearts.

The door of Heavens

Saint Peter forgot to close the door
And I could listen to the music which swept me off my feet.
I guess it was Markos (Vanvakaris) who played bouzouki
And Stelios was singing the song of poverty.
Hiotis was there with Manolis (Aggelopoulos)
Who sang "your black eyes" and everybody cried.
Stratos rose up and sang the song "Paliatzis"
And then people tore down the store of Hades.
The angels stood up and danced Zeibekiko dance
And everybody their life's memories on earth.

The first song I heard from Dimitris Xanthakis was the "Mailman":

By Dimitrios K. Kakavitsas

"*Mailman, don't knock on the door,*
Nobody will open the door for you,
Disaster knocked down my poor home.
Here that love was dwelling,
Now the pain has built its palace"

Figure 29 - The Author with his favorite signer, Dimitri Xanthaki

I was very impressed by the talent and the sweet-
ness of his voice. He sang like no one else could sing. He
was and still is unique. His songs are odd and different,
like: "No more red lips, they pierce like thorns of a wild
rose," "It's raining in the poor neighborhood," The old
glories," "Odd-Even," "You are a rare beauty" and many
other songs which became very successful.

That's how in 1989 he recorded his last disc in which all the songs are exceptionally good : "My child, be careful," "It's getting dark," "The night bird," "You ask me to forget you," "Come again to my dreams," "Whatever you ask and whatever you say,"

I put Dimitris Xanthakis in my heart, next to Stelios Kazantzidis. I was looking for him everywhere. I wanted to meet him and listen to him singing live. I tried very hard, but I couldn't find him.

In 1979, I was in Agrinio. My sister called me and said: "Are you still looking for Xanthakis? He is singing at Can-Can."

"I'm coming," I said. "Let's go listen to him."

We got together some good friends and went to the tavern where he sang. It was hard to get in the tavern but I gave a big tip and we were given a table in the first row. I ordered plates and flowers and waited for my beloved singer. I was waiting until 2 am and Xanthakis never came. Then I asked the owner of the tavern what happened to Xanthakis and he said; "Xanthakis is not here today, he quit the tavern yesterday."

So I asked him why Xanthakis' name was still on the tavern sign outside.

"I didn't have time to take it off," he said.

Another time I went to Athens to see Xanthakis again. Once I got in the tavern, something happened and the club closed before I could even find a seat. I heard half of a song and I had to go.

In 1985, I was in Athens and a friend of mine told me: "If you still want to see Xanthakis, he sings in the tavern of Karapateas."

I went with him to the tavern immediately. After we found our seats, I was thinking to myself that something would go wrong. I was very anxious and I couldn't believe that I would see Dimitris face to face. In a while, I saw Xanthakis come out on stage and I stood right in front of him. I hugged him and told him that I wanted to talk to him. With a gentle smile he said "all right." I gave him my request and he sang a song:

"I want to spread my wings like the eagle,

To fly above the hatred of the world.

To look at the world from the clouds,

And to end up resting at the house of your love,

What if people gave me bitter drinks?

I'm born an eagle and I'll remain an eagle.

I want to grab in my claws

Those who torture people.

So the people who suffer will find joy

And I'll destroy the powerful ones who separate us,

I didn't believe that I was in the real world and everything felt like a dream. Afterwards, Xanthakis came over to our table and I asked him for his telephone number and address. He gave them to me and since then we are like brothers. At least, that's how I feel. I believe that's how he feels as well and he shows it to me every time we get together.

Whenever I go to Greece, he always honors me with his presence wherever I go. When I called him and told him that I have to go to prison for two years, it sounded like he couldn't speak from his sadness.

Figure 30 - The Author giving flowers to another of his favorite singers in Greece, Stratos Dionisiou - 1975

My life with wrestlers

In 1967, when I came from Greece to Charlotte, North Carolina, the first Monday I was here someone took me to see wrestling. At every move they made, I was closing my eyes. I was scared and I always felt bad for them because they were beating up on each other.

'Til today I never miss live wrestling live or on TV. This is the reason I have a lot of wrestling friends. I show them my admiration and they respect me as well.

In my restaurant I have a lot of pictures of them. Seventy-five percent of my customers look over the pictures and appreciate them. I love these athletes very much. I like the way they talk. They use simple language that everyone can understand.

When I was in prison, I received a lot of letters from them. They gave me hope and strength to make it through.

All the inmates would come to my cell to look at my pictures. I want to thank every one of my wrestler friends from the bottom of my heart for the happiness and strength they gave me.

Figure 31 - The Author with Ric Flair

Figure 32 - The Author with Chris Jericho

Laughter Causes No Harm

Let's leave the painful stuff for a while and say some words about laughter. Laughter is God's gift to humans. Only evil people and beasts don't laugh. The person who laughs shows the purity of their heart. The people who hide malice inside of them cannot laugh. Jokes, though, should be gentle and polite, so that all people might enjoy them and laugh.

If something bad happens, smile. The doctors say laughter is healthy. The following jokes are polite and don't insult your dignity:

Karagiozis, hungry as usual, passes outside of a palace and sees a servant at the window.

"Servant!" He shouts. "Throw me a pin."

"How can I throw it to you, Karagiozis, it will get lost?" said the servant.

"Well, nail it to a loaf of bread so it won't get lost,"

Karagiozis said.

A lazy guy had a coin in his hands. Every now and then he tossed it up and said, "If it lands on heads, I'll go to the tavern. If it lands on tails, I'll go to bed. And, if it stands up, I'll go to work."

A woman said to one of her girl-friends,

"Now that both of my daughters are married, I don't know which one I should go and stay with: To the one that lives in Athens or the one in Patra? Both of my sons-in-law insist so much."

"I guess your sons-in-law love you very much," her friend said.

A little boy asks his mother,

"Why do you have some white hairs?"

"This happens when somebody has disobedient children like you," his mother replied.

"Now I understood why my grandmother's hair is totally white," the little boy said.

Proverbs

• The greedy person has endless needs.

• It's better to have a horrible end, instead of having a horrible life without an end.

• The way you give something matters more than what you give.

• War is the science of disaster.

• Never bite the hand that has helped you.

• You love a worthless person when you love an ungrateful one.

• Saving money is the biggest income.

• The most useless day is the day you don't laugh.

My Last Hours in Prison

My friends, the big moment came today, April 17th, at 7am. After I said "good-bye" to all of my friends and staff in prison, I went to the prison office. When I arrived they gave me a box with clothes my family had sent me. When I opened the box and touched clothes, I got goose bumps. I put them on and I left the office.

After I passed the prison gate and walked towards my freedom, I saw my son, Vasilis, who was waiting for me and I felt like I was losing my mind. On my way back home everything looked beautiful, the houses, the streets, the lights, all those were pieces of real paradise. My son's cell phone was ringing all the time and everyone wanted to talk to me. My excitement was great and I had tears in my eyes on the way home. After 2 to 3 hours we arrived at home.

All of my relatives and friends were there waiting for me. It was a great day and a great joy for me.

I thank you all from the bottom of my heart and I wish all of you the best.

By Dimitrios G. Kakavitsas

Epilogue

I don't apologize for anything I've done in my life because I have never harmed a single soul.

The people who apologize show signs of guilt. If I have to apologize to somebody, it's only to God. I should apologize to Him for any failure to do good deeds or speak good things.

I believe that He will judge and He might condemn me, because I am His creature and His child!

To those who say that I spend a lot of money and that I don't care about 'tomorrow' I say that in their concern about 'tomorrow' they don't see 'today' which slides under their feet. They look like those people who are being described by the folkloric song:

The people who collect money accomplish what?
They die and not even a penny
To take with them!

I truly believe that we, the people who came to foreign lands, did that to improve the conditions of our life, to overcome poverty and to earn the 'today'.

The 'today' includes our family, our relatives and most of all, our friends, and for them we should sacrifice everything without any second thought.

We came to America in order to work hard, to experience the Freedom, the Justice and Equality. To live the excitement which our country denied us, this is the education of our children, the humanity and the life of 'today.'

America is the best country in the world – except for its justice system. If we are ever able to repair it, then America will be the greatest country of all time.

Figure 33 - The biggest day in the Author's life - arriving home on April 17, 2006 after his release from prison.

Figure 34 - The Author kissing the driveway of his home

Figure 35 - The Author at home with his wife

Figure 36 - The Author inside of his home with relatives

Figure 37 - The Author outside his house with his special friends

Figure 38 - The Author with his brother and his brother's wife and kids

Figure 39 - The Author with his favorite friends playing their favorite music.
Welcome back to his music

Figure 40 - The Author with his lovely cousins

Figure 41 - The Author with his son and friend listening to their favorite music

Figure 42 - The Author with his favorite friend, Chris Spirou – 2008

Figure 43 - The Author with his two nieces

Figure 44 - The Author was campaigning for Hillary Clinton in 2008

COMMUNITY NEWS

Announcing

All Children's Christmas Party
Food, Drinks and Gifts
Santa Clause will arrive with his helicopter
December 23rd, 2009 at 3:00 pm
at Skyland Restaurant
=======================

Dear Reporter for the Community-at-large;
Once again, we bother you (as of the THANKSGIVING event),
and inform you of our 2nd (second) Annual event; CHILDREN!

Two days before Christmas, we invite ALL youngsters to come
to our Restaurant for a GRAND CHRISTMAS PARTY: FREE food,
drinks and gifts, and we'll bring SANTA CLAUS with Helicopter
in our Parking lot -- as we did it last year.

I know you love children; and we too love those little
angels and we want to make them happy.... after all, "Isn't
Christmas CHILDREN'S HOLLY DAY"...

P L E A S E , MAKE AN ANNOUNCEMENT ON YOUR MEDIA, THAT THE
CHRISTMAS PARTY WILL TAKE PLACE AT SKYLAND'S RESTAURANT ON
SOUTH BLVD FROM 3:00 - 6:00 pm + ALL invited. Let them
bring their Cameras to take photos with Santa at his Helicopter.

GRATEFULLY YOURS,

Jimmy Kakaritsas

4544 South Boulevard • Charlotte, NC 28209, USA • Phone: 704-522-6522 • Fax: 704-522-6523

228

Figure 45 - The Author with Santa at a special Christmas Party

Figure 46 - The Author, his two sons and the Priest

Figure 47 - The Author with kids at the special Christmas Party

Table of Figures